Seashells

Seashells
A Photographic Celebration

N.R. GORDON

MALLARD PRESS

An imprint of BDD Promotional Book Company, Inc.
666 Fifth Avenue
New York, New York 10103

A FRIEDMAN GROUP BOOK

Published by MALLARD PRESS
An imprint of BDD Promotional Book Company, Inc.
666 Fifth Avenue
New York, New York 10103

Mallard Press and its accompanying design and logo are trademarks
of BDD Promotional Book Company, Inc.

ISBN 0-792-45263-1

SEASHELLS
was prepared and produced by
Michael Friedman Publishing Group, Inc.
15 West 26th Street
New York, New York 10010

Art Director: Jeff Batzli
Designer: Devorah Levinrad
Photography Editor: Christopher Bain
Photo Researcher: Daniella Jo Nilva
Production: Karen L. Greenberg

Typeset by BPE Graphics, Inc.
Color separations by Universal Colour Scanning, Ltd.
Printed and bound in Hong Kong by Leefung-Asco Printers Ltd.

FOR JOHN

The author gratefully acknowledges the following authors and publishers:

"The Oyster and the Litigants" by Jean de la Fontaine, translated by James Michie, from LA FONTAINE: *Selected Fables,* (Penguin Classics, 1982), copyright © James Michie, 1979, reprinted with permission from Penguin Books Ltd.

"The Oyster" by Ogden Nash, from MANY LONG YEARS AGO, copyright © Ogden Nash, 1931, reprinted with permission from Little, Brown and Company.

"The Clam" by Ogden Nash, from EVERYONE BUT THEE AND ME, copyright © Ogden Nash, 1962, renewed 1986 by Frances Nash, Isabel Nash Eberstadt, and Linnell Nash Smith, reprinted with permission from Little, Brown and Company.

"Poem in October" by Dylan Thomas, copyright © 1945 by the Trustees for the Copyright of Dylan Thomas, reprinted with permission from New Directions Publishing Corporation.

"Anthem for St. Cecilia's Day" by W.H. Auden, from W.H. AUDEN: *Collected Works,* edited by Edward Mendelson, copyright © 1945 by W.H. Auden, reprinted with permission from Random House, Inc.

CONTENTS

GLOSSARY
page 8

INTRODUCTION
page 10

Part One
UNIVALVES
page 28

Part Two
BIVALVES
page 102

SHELL CLUBS
page 142

FOR FURTHER READING
page 143

INDEX
page 144

GLOSSARY

APERTURE
In gastropods and tusk shells, an opening through which the mollusk's head and foot protrude.

BODY WHORL
In gastropods, the last of the whorls to be produced. It is usually the largest whorl and contains most of the soft body parts.

BYSSUS
Horny or coarse thread that serves to attach some species of bivalves to solid objects.

CALCAREOUS
Made of calcium carbonate [$CaCo_3$], a compound naturally found in shells; also limy or shelly.

COLUMELLA
The solid or hollow pillarlike axis around which the whorls of some gastropods coil.

INTERTIDAL
The area between the high- and low-tide lines.

MANTLE
The fleshy lobe or lobes that line shells and typically secrete the shelly material; the mantle contains the mollusk's visceral organs.

NACRE
Mother-of-pearl; layer of iridescent shell.

NUCLEAR WHORL
In gastropods, the first whorl to be made.

OPERCULUM
In some gastropods, a circle of shelly or horny material on the back part of the animal's foot that serves as a trap door when the animal pulls itself into its shell.

PERIOSTRACUM
An outer covering on the shell, either smooth or fibrous.

RADIAL RIBBING
In bivalves, sculptural ridges in the shell that extend from the umbones out.

RADULA
A ribbonlike organ with tiny teeth located in the mouth and used in feeding.

SPIRE
In gastropods, all of the whorls produced before the body whorl.

UMBO(NES)
In bivalves, the first part of the shell to be produced, located above the hinge.

WHORL
One full coil of the shell in spirally oriented gastropods.

I have seen

A curious child, who dwelt upon a tract

Of inland ground applying to his ear

The convolutions of a smooth-lipped shell;

To which, in silence hushed, his very soul

Listened intensely; and his countenance soon

Brightened with joy; for from within were heard

Murmurings, whereby the monitor expressed

Mysterious union with its native sea.

  William Wordsworth

  "Extempore Effusion upon the Death of James Hogg"

INTRODUCTION

To many of us the myth of the shell begins with the roar of the sea. We listen, like the curious child, with our souls, and the ocean approaches. With shell to our ear, we feel the sea's cool mist, its pungent smell, and the peculiar scratch of sand between our toes, even if we sit hundreds of miles away in a moldy attic. The sound is full of stories—of mermaids using spined shells for combs, of goddesses rising from the sea on shells, of saints and sorcerers offering shells as protection—stories that cast an enchanting spell on those who still appreciate a little wonder in their lives.

What is a seashell that it has such power over us? In unromantic terms, it is the calcareous covering of a saltwater mollusk. Which means, roughly, that the shell that generates so much awe is essentially a layered structure of calcium carbonate, which familiarly is a type of lime. An animal—a mollusk—produces the shell as it grows.

To say that a mollusk is an invertebrate animal that belongs to the phylum Mollusca probably doesn't mean much to the average beginning shell connoisseur, especially if one's high school biology has faded from memory. A phylum is simply an organizational group that biologists use to distinguish animals or plants that share some of the same characteristics. Man, for example, belongs to the Animal kingdom, the phylum Chordata, the order Primates, the family Hominidae, the genus *Homo,* and the species *sapiens.* Mollusks also belong to the Animal kingdom, but there they depart from man. Yet the phylum Mollusca—with an estimated 50,000 to 100,000 species—should not be unfamiliar; it includes the octopuses and squid, as well as clams, oysters, and sea snails.

All mollusks have a soft body with no backbone; internal organs; a foot used for locomotion or attachment; and, except for the bivalves, a head. Some even have eyes, a proboscis, and a mouth that contains not a tongue but a fine-toothed radula, a ribbonlike structure used to gather and tear up food.

Avid shellers will crouch for hours watching the goings-on of what photographer Andreas Feininger affectionately calls "an apparently insignificant lump of animated slime." The internal organs remain hidden in this slime. What observers tend to see, if they see anything at all, are the head, the foot and the fascinating mantle that typically secretes the shelly material and extends out from the body wall, which surrounds the visceral mass where the body organs are located.

Although the phylum Mollusca encompasses seven major classes, most shellers are interested in only five: Polyplacophora, Gastropoda, Bivalvia, Scaphopoda, and Cephalopoda.

Chitons

The marine chitons of the class Polyplacophora are the most primitive group of mollusks. Eight overlapping plates, or valves, make up the chiton's shell, giving it a flexibility that allows the animal to roll up in a ball like a wood louse. A cartilaginous girdle surrounds the plates and keeps them together. Collectors rarely look for or exhibit chitons; they are the ugly ducklings of the molluscan world.

CHITONS, SUCH AS THESE SPLEN-did Chitons *(Ischnochiton res-plendens),* are the most primitive group of mollusks. They first appeared in the ar-chaeological record about 550 million years ago.

ALTHOUGH THE CHITON'S SHELLY plates serve as a protective barrier against predators, the mollusk can also roll up into a tight ball when disturbed. The chitons pictured here come from the Sea of Cortez in Baja, California.

Gastropods

Gastropods, on the other hand, are often shellers' pieces of eight. No matter where they come from or how dirty they are at first, once gastropods are cleaned, they become personal treasures. And, although the value of most shells lies in the soul of the collector, some of the rarest marine gastropods have fetched more than a thousand dollars at auction.

Gastropod means "stomach-footed," a term that describes these creatures' peculiar mode of locomotion; they crawl about not on their stomachs, as many other invertebrate animals do, but on their muscular foot. Over the ages the oceans couldn't contain these hardy creatures, which have also found niches in fresh water and on land. The marine gastropod species maintain gills that allow them to survive underwater, in some cases to depths of more than five thousand feet.

Also called univalves, these sea creatures produce a single shell that, with some exceptions, becomes larger as it spirals away from its central axis, or columella. The variations within the realm of these spirals—from the simple slit shells to the glossy cowries and cones to the intricate conchs and Murex shells—attract a loyal cadre of univalve devotees.

THE DEFINITIVE COILED SHAPE of a gastropod is easily seen in these slender Marlinspikes *(Terebra maculata)* of the Indo-Pacific.

© Alex Kerstitch

© Alex Kerstitch

THE BEAUTIFUL MANTLE OF THE Flamingo Tongue *(Cyphoma gibbosum)* (above) upstages the shell it covers. Found in shallow water on sea fans and sea whips, the snail can be collected off shore from North Carolina to Brazil.

FROM THIS SIDE UP, THE BLEED-ing Tooth Snail *(Nerita pe-loronta* or *Theodoxus leutofas-ciatus)* (left) hides its trademark "tooth." These specimens from western Mex-ico, however, illustrate the subtle variations found within a single species.

Bivalves

The pelecypods, or bivalves, tend to attract fewer collectors than the gastropods, but men have feasted on bivalves since prehistoric times. Ancient garbage heaps, which archaeologists dub kitchen middens, reveal layer upon layer of shells such as clams, oysters, and scallops, which are all bivalves. Two shells, or valves, protect the soft inner bodies of these animals. When danger nears, the animal can shut itself inside. A foot propels many species along the ocean bottom, while some use water pressure to jet around and others cling to solid surfaces by means of horny threads called a byssus.

Scaphopods

Denizens of the deep, most scaphopods live far beyond the range of sport divers and unsophisticated dredgers. This inaccessibility and the scaphopods' simplicity—they are the simplest of all mollusks—keep most shell aficionados away. Their tusklike shape attracted some cultures to use scaphopod shells for money and decoration (see also page 56). Unlike other members of its class, the tusk shell has no gills.

TUSK SHELLS OF THE CLASS Scaphopoda represent only about 350 living species. Many of these primarily deep-water animals live partially submerged in sandy or muddy bottoms in depths below 100 feet (30 m).

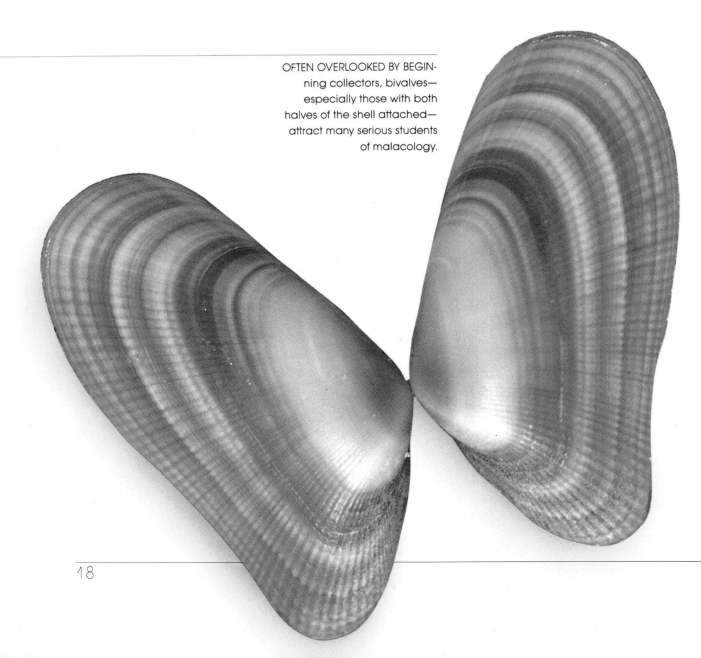

OFTEN OVERLOOKED BY BEGIN-ning collectors, bivalves—especially those with both halves of the shell attached—attract many serious students of malacology.

Cephalopods

Only one cephalopod usually makes its way into beginning shellers' homes, yet it is one that captures the imagination: the nautilus. The nautilus seduces its admirers with a relatively large, stunning creamy shell marked with almost feline brownish or reddish stripes. Less than half a dozen nautilus species exist, all in the cooler, deeper waters off islands in the tropical Pacific. An explosion of interest in the past decade revealed many of this complex mollusk's secrets. But even before this new wave of interest, Jules Verne memorialized his respect for the animal by naming Captain Nemo's ship *The Nautilus*.

For years biologists and physicists have puzzled over a miracle of natural engineering unsuspected by the casual observer; the unusual way the nautilus maintains and changes its buoyancy through gaseous secretions that fill its empty chambers. Most people likewise appreciate the nautilus's fine form. Most do not realize, however, that mathematicians have long prized the nautilus's beautifully proportioned spiraled shells as an organic example of elegant number series or proportions such as the Fibonacci Sequence or the Golden Section (based on relationships between numbers and proportions that are crucial to some aspects of the Western aesthetic sensibility). Perhaps more than any other shell the nautilus's beauty goes beyond that of a beautiful bauble; it is a reminder of order in the universe.

The nautilus shares its position as a member of the cephalopod order with shelless octopuses and squid and with the odd argonaut, which produces a papery shell.

THE MYSTERY AND BEAUTY OF the Nautilus is legendary. These captivating creatures have relatively well-developed sense organs—including large eyes—and a brain. Neurologists study its unusual nerve fibers, hoping to gain insight into the human nerve system.

THE SPIRAL OF A NAUTILUS shell, here shown in cross section, increases in diameter exactly three times with each successive turn.

Collecting and Conservation

Ocean life has not escaped the ravages of pollution. As man continues to pump pesticides and other chemicals, heated water, and trash into seawater, the animals and plants it harbors suffer. Oil spills, siltation from shoreside construction and inland farms, even scuba divers can harm the sensitive flora and fauna underwater. Mollusks suffer along with the sea otters, whales, shorebirds, and other animals that receive more publicity.

Shelled animals, especially in the tropics, must survive not just pollution but blatantly unwise fishing practices. To get at tropical fish for aquariums, at shells for collectors, and sometimes at fish to take to market, people are poisoning coral reefs with bleach, cyanide, and other chemicals; blast-ing the water with dynamite to recover fish not irretrievably damaged; and simply poaching. These degradations are signals that as shell connoisseurs we must respect the habitats of the animals we admire. As a beginning sheller, take a notebook and pen to the water and keep a journal of your observations. Pick up shells to look at the living animals, but replace them before leaving. "Dead" shells litter many beaches, and although these may not have the sheen or perfection of "live" shells, they are interesting too because they force collectors to become aware of the environment, of tides and storms, and of the flux of populations: A little bit of study enables collectors to judge the best times to pick up "dead" shells.

RESPONSIBLE COLLECTORS DISturb as little of the shell's habitat as possible. In fact, many shellers take as much pleasure from "dead" shells—shells that have washed ashore—as they do from shells with living animals inside. These "dead" shells from Sanibel Island, Florida, are a little more bleached and smoother than live shells, but they are just as fascinating.

The Gallery of Shells

Use this book not as a field guide or collector's manual but as a gallery of great art—a showcase of gastropod and bivalve shells. Because of the complexity of modern taxonomy (the classification of plants and animals), the shells within these pages are grouped roughly by family from the most primitive to the most complex. Many families—primarily those whose appeal to collectors is minimal—are left out; and some families that are included are presented together with other families because of their similarities. The choice of common name is largely subjective, although I owe great thanks to the organization of—and to the author and editors of—*The Audubon Society Field Guide to North American Seashells,* and to R. Tucker Abbott, whose many books on shells are not only invaluable resources but also a pleasure to read.

This book is meant only to pique the curiosity of the individuals who must stop to pick up a pretty shell on the beach, of those who listen for the ocean and hear the orchestra of nature. Many of the shells tell a story—in their beauty, their history, or their interaction with man. Heed their messages, and like the curious child, discover the mysterious union humankind can share with the sea.

COLLECTORS RATE SHELLS AC-cording to their maturity, cleanliness, and wear, cate-gorizing them as *fine, good, poor,* and *juvenile.* These, probably classed as "beach specimens," were found off Sanibel Island, Florida.

SHELL COLLECTIONS

The earliest shell collectors predate our written history. It wasn't until the Renaissance, however, that men and women began collecting in earnest. The seafarers of that Age of Exploration opened the world to Europeans, who by the Elizabethan era had constructed elaborate shell grottoes—entire rooms "wallpapered" with shells—and left behind shell-adorned artifacts.

Today, the art and pleasure of collecting lies not only in gathering an assemblage of the rarest species, but in learning about the shells. Technology and capitalism have brought more shells to market and, in turn, driven down prices.

Collectors adapted to these changes, and the emphasis now in many shell collectors' clubs is on local or regional collections; family or genus collections; or specialized collections that show the growth cycle of a species, for instance, or a series of albino shells.

Serious collectors do still pay hundreds and sometimes thousands of dollars for perfect, rare specimens, but this is the exception to the rule. Beginning collectors most often pick up shells themselves, or trade with other beginners, or pay the twenty-five to fifty cents that most species command in the marketplace.

TO BEGIN A COLLECTION, NOTE down the place where the shell was found, its habitat, the date of collection, and if desired, the price paid or value of the shell. Shell displays reflect the collector's intent: This collection comes from a casual beachcomber rather than an amateur scientist.

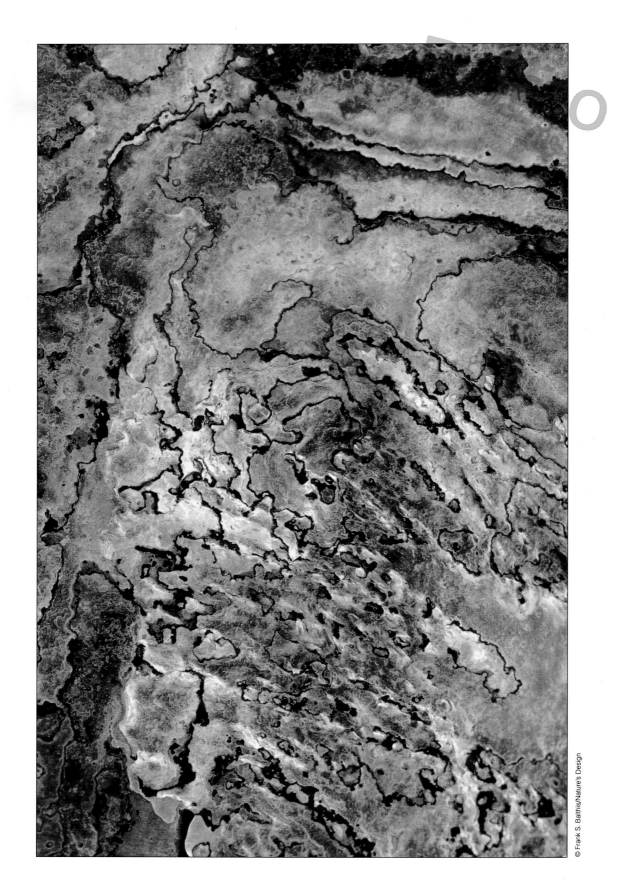

Part One

UNIVALVES

SLIT SHELLS

(PLEUROTOMARIIDAE)

In 1855 a fisherman in the French West Indies accidentally caught a hermit crab that had snatched a slit shell, *Pleurotomaria quoyana,* from deeper waters. The find raised eyebrows among conchologists: Up to that point scientists had agreed that the family Pleurotomariidae was extinct—and had been for approximately five or six hundred years. Since the discovery of *Pleurotomaria quoyana,* only a dozen or so species have come to light, and all are considered prize treasures, primarily because the reclusive mollusks inhabit the ocean at depths of up to 350 feet (105 m).

When examined even superficially, the shells reveal a slit on the last whorl that serves as a primitive means of expelling waste water. The top shape recalls turban shells; their interiors generally shine with the iridescence of mother-of-pearl.

NATURE—NOT A COMPUTER— enhanced this photograph of an abalone shell's interior. Its extraordinary iridescence has made it a valued material for craftspeople through the ages.

ABALONE

(HALIOTIDAE)

Irrespective of the abalone's usefulness, man has had a long love affair with this creature. The interior shells of abalone gleam with a rainbow-colored iridescence that shimmers much like oil on water. For centuries man crafted the shell first into necklaces and inlays, then into buttons and more sophisticated jewelry. The abalone's beauty helped it find its way along ancient trade routes deep into the southwestern United States, where the shell has turned up as decoration on Zuni kachina dolls, most likely as a symbol of the sacred water used to irrigate corn.

Even though the abalone family consists of almost a hundred species worldwide, the most common representatives in the United States, found off the California coast, are now subject to harvest restrictions because of overfishing. The largest American species, *Haliotis rufescens,* or Red Abalone, can grow up to 1 foot (30.5 cm) long and is the most commercially valuable member of the family.

Called ormers, or ear shells, because its shape somewhat resembles an ear, the abalone's most notable exterior characteristic is a row of holes along one edge of the shell. The abalone expels water through these holes after its gills have filtered out the oxygen.

THE RED ABALONE TAKES ITS name from the shell's rufous-hued exterior.

KEYHOLE LIMPETS

(FISSURELLIDAE)

Most keyhole limpets look like oval-shaped caps with their top point lopped off leaving a small hole for excretion. Some of these shells are ribbed, and others are not. The Volcano Limpet, *Fissurella volcano*—a California native—has reddish streaks that, with a little imagination, resemble a fresh lava flow; some specimens show a ring of red around the hole, making the analogy even more apt. In Colombia, the highland Saha people offered *Fissurella nimbosa* as a gift to the spirit of the snowy mountains; here again, the shells' conical peaks reminded them of the mountains.

The almost celadon interior of the Barbados Keyhole Limpet *(Fissurella barbadensis)* makes its shell a pretty find off southeastern Florida, where collectors must look beyond the algae to find it. (Limpet shells—both keyhole and true—attract algae, which acts as camouflage.)

Most of the hundred-odd North American species measure between ½ inch (1.3 cm) and 2 inches (5 cm) tall and vary from 1 inch (2.5 cm) to 4 inches (10.2 cm) in length. Rarer, smaller species exist in deep water.

With no operculum (a horny plate that closes off the shells of many gastropods) to protect itself, keyhole limpets cling to rocks with fierce attachment. If you watch closely as a keyhole limpet breathes, you will see it lift itself away from its rock with a very subtle motion.

THE MANTLE OF THIS GIANT KEY-
hole Limpet *(Megathura
crenulata)* disguises the shell's
caplike shape.

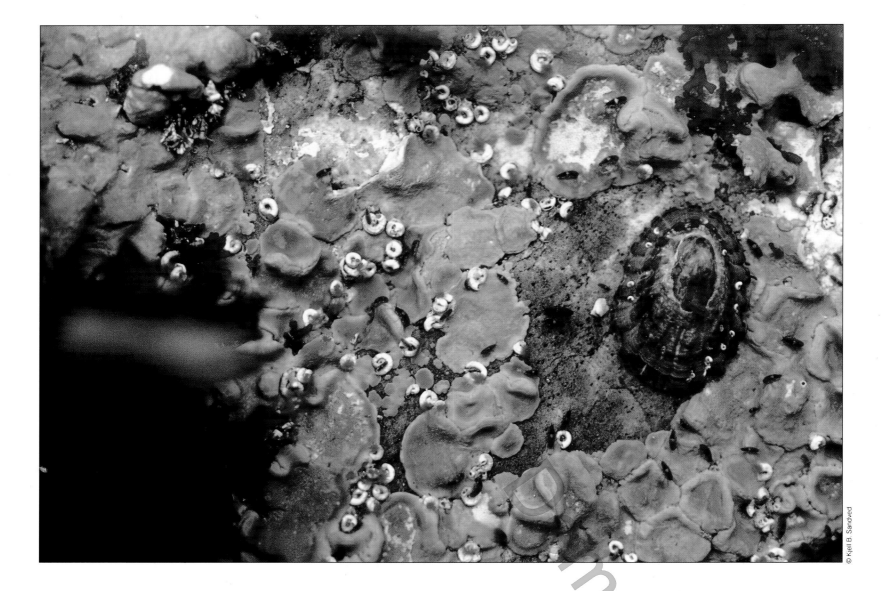

SHALLOW-WATER LIMPETS CAN often be found in intertidal pools. This Falkland Island species shares its habitat with tubeworms.

TRUE LIMPETS
(ACMAEIDAE AND PATELLIDAE)

Cap-shaped like keyhole limpets, true limpets don't have a hole or slit. Their pointy tops and broad contours inspired many names within the family; Acmaeidae, for instance, derives from the Greek word for point *(akme),* while some of the species' names describe a shield, a cap, or a tortoise shell. Although the exterior shells of true limpets can be covered with algae or a coating of limy material, the interior linings usually present a handsome face, often with a dark, contrasting center spot amid a pearly white background.

Most true limpets live within the intertidal zone—the area between the high- and low-tide lines—off rocky shores from the United States (East and West coasts, Alaska, and Hawaii) to New Zealand. Malacologist and author R. Tucker Abbott dubbed South Africa, another hunting ground, "limpet heaven."

Favorite shells among collectors include the tortoise-shell–trimmed Atlantic Plate Limpet *(Notoacmaea testudinalis)* and the largest North American limpet, the Giant Owl Limpet *(Lottia gigantea),* which, when polished, appears in markets as jewelry.

NOT KNOWN FOR THEIR ASTON-
ishing colors, the shells of the
limpet family do include a few
notable exceptions: The Dark-
lined Limpet *(Patella nigro-
lineata)* is one.

TOP SHELLS
(TROCHIDAE)

This large family of more than 1,000 species embraces about 150 species in North American waters alone. The flesh, while tasty to some people, has never taken off commercially, although a few of the pearly shells have been used for buttons.

A yellowish-orange shell with bright purple-pink bands, the Ringed Top Shell (Calliostoma annulatum) is one of the most beautiful in the family; also called the Purple-Ringed Top Shell, the approximately 1-inch (2.5-cm) high shell thrives amid kelp or rocks along the West Coast from Alaska to the Baja peninsula. A smaller beauty, the North Atlantic Top Shell (Calliostoma occidentale), reveals a pearly iridescence when clean. It grows to about ½ inch (1.3 cm) and is slightly broader than its western cousin. The Jujube Top Shell (Calliostoma jujubinum), with its delicate beading, captivates many casual shellers from North Carolina southward, where it frequently washes up on beaches. Its nickname, Mottled Top Shell, comes from subtle white splotches that give the Jujube a gracefulness lacking in more static-looking shells.

In contrast, the West Indian Top Shell (Cittarium pica) can, when mature, grow to more than 4 inches (10.2 cm) in height and width. Far from being a delicate shell, its bold black, white, and yellowish patterning looks strangely feline. Unlike the pearly or bold top shells, the Superb Gaza (Gaza superba), a wider shell, often requires a second glance for collectors to appreciate its comeliness. The green-brown shell appears almost nondescript until the light picks up the greenish and pinkish iridescence that makes it so special. Like other deep dwellers, the Superb Gaza comes up in dredges only occasionally and so is a worthy collectible.

THE GENUS NAME FOR THE Granulose Top Shell (Calliostoma supragranosum) is derived from Greek for "beautiful mouth," a reference to the shell's pearly opening. Found on rocky shores at low tide, the shell's range extends from Monterey to Baja, California.

© James McFalls

THE WEST INDIAN TOP SHELL
once inhabited rocky shores
off the coast of Florida; its
range today is restricted to the
West Indies. Its demise in
American waters may be due
in part to its tasty meat.

TURBAN, STAR, AND PHEASANT SHELLS
(TURBINIDAE)

Probably the most interesting—and largest—of the turban shells is the Green Turban Shell *(Turbo marmoratus)*, which grows to approximately 8 inches (20.3 cm) in the waters of Southeast Asia. The contemporary artists of Taiwan who carve designs deep into the surface of the shells follow in the footsteps of others who have valued the Green Turban Shell for its unusual beauty. The Chambri people of New Guinea, who exchanged *T. marmoratus* specifically for food or tobacco, accepted the challenge of arguing the merits of each individual specimen. Color, sheen, and size all gave individual shells a unique personality; in addition, the Chambri assigned a gender to each specimen. The history and physical characteristics combined to give each shell a value that had to be established anew every time the shell traded hands.

In the Philippines, the Ifugo men held the operculum of the Green Turban in high esteem, making the plate into half-dollar–size disks to thread into spiritually protective belts. Because the shielding operculum hinders enemies from entering the shell, it came to symbolize male-oriented gods.

The Green Turban's cousin, the Pacific Tapestry Turban *(Turbo petholatus)*, commands attention primarily for its glossy, blue-green operculum rather than its shell. This "cat's eye" operculum looks like a semiprecious gem and is often made into necklaces, bracelets, or rings.

With an estimated 500 species, the turban family varies from shells of less than ⅛ inch (.3 cm) to upward of 1 foot

SCHOLARS DO NOT YET KNOW whether the spines of star shells are splendid accidents of nature or protective armor. These Triumphant Stars are also known as Victorious Turbans. The triumph for serious collectors is to find a specimen in perfect condition.

(30.5 cm). Its common genus name *Turbo* comes from the Latin word for "spinning top," appropriate because, when viewed in profile, many of the shells do indeed recall the shape of a child's toy top.

The beautiful star shells share the same toplike shape. From a head-on perspective, the pretty Long-Spined Star Shell *(Astraea phoebia)* delivers a good argument for its common name; its spines jut out to form a multipointed star. Found in southern Florida and the Caribbean, it rivals its East Asian relatives, the Triumphant Star *(Guildfordia triumphans)* and the Yoka Star *(Guildfordia yoka)*, which log in at 3 to 4 inches (7.6 to 10.2 cm) across and have less plentiful but longer spikes. The plainer *Astraea heliotropium* of New Zealand has no rays to flaunt. Rather, it boasts a stunning rainbow iridescence that has been compared to stained glass.

Biologists who classify and order animal species are often called *lumpers* or *splitters*, depending upon their tendency to place similar animals together or in their own category. Pheasant shells fall under the family Phasianellidae in some texts, while in others they are found under Turbinidae. However they are grouped, these shiny (but not pearly) shells tend to be small (⅛ to ½ inch [.3 to 1.3 cm]) in North America and larger (up to 3 inches [7.6 cm]) in the warmer waters of southern Australia. The Australian species are quite handsome, bearing shells of earthy green, tan, brown, and orange—much like the colors of a pheasant.

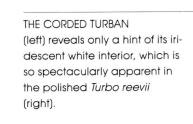

THE CORDED TURBAN
(left) reveals only a hint of its iridescent white interior, which is so spectacularly apparent in the polished *Turbo reevii* (right).

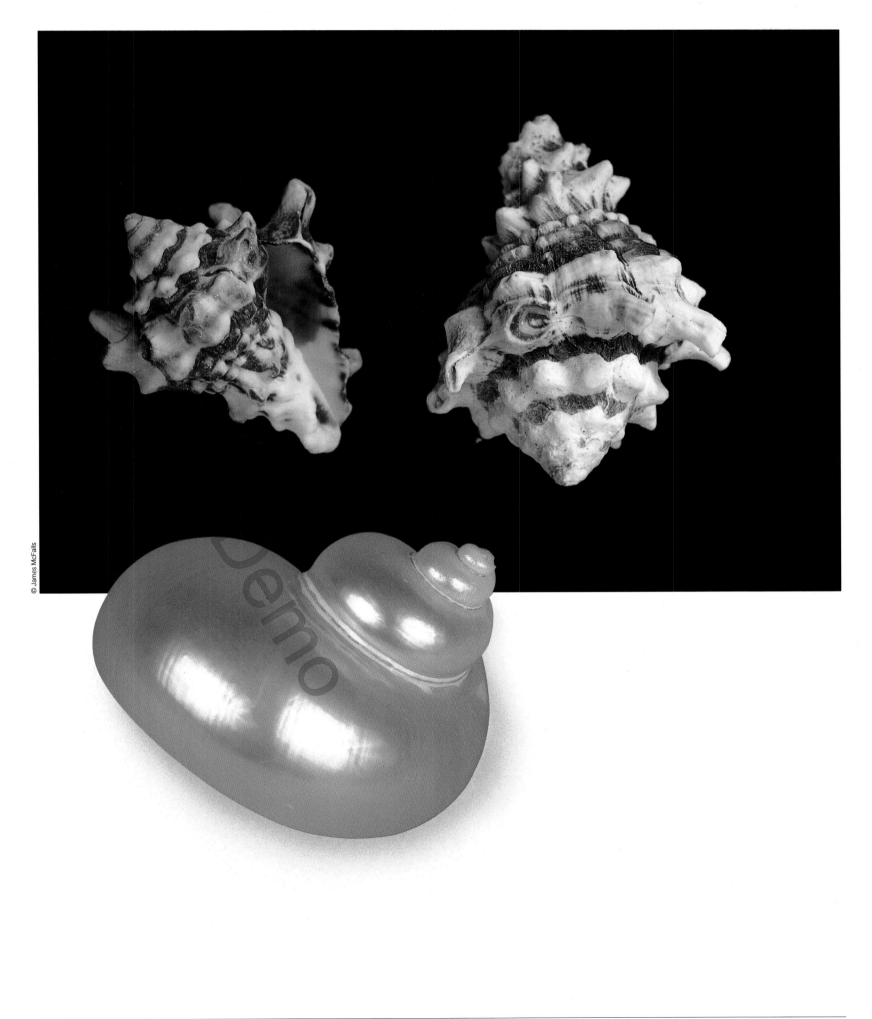

NERITES

(NERITIDAE)

The word *Nerite* refers to the Roman sea god Nereus, the Old Man of the Sea, who gave birth to the sea-nymphs, the Nereids. Several hundred species of Nerite shells populate the world's oceans, but fewer than twenty live off of North American shores.

The celebrity of the Nerite family is undoubtedly the Bleeding Tooth *(Nerita peloronta)*, a roughly rounded shell with irregular black and rust zigzags set against a creamy background. The animal's peculiar name, however, comes not from its topshell but from its two white "teeth" on the shell's underside. A scarlet splotch above the teeth brings its name to life. The Four-Toothed, or Variegated, Nerite *(Nerita versicolor)* also sports an open-mouthed, toothy smile. Both prefer exposed rocks between the high- and low-tide lines and range from southern Florida to the West Indies. The Zebra Nerite *(Puperita pupa)*, another famous family member with the same distribution, lures collectors to the subtropics. Its arresting stripes are worthy of its common name.

Nature plays with variation to a remarkable degree within the species *Neritina virginea*, the Virgin Nerite. The contrasting dark-and-light patterns are a fabric designer's treasure trove and a collector's delight.

NERITINAS, LIKE THESE FROM THE Pacific side of Panama (far left), illustrate the remarkable variation found within some species of shells. Tolerant Neritinas, which naturally occur in brackish mangrove lagoons, are not so tolerant that they can survive manmade pollution.

PERIWINKLES

(LITTORINIDAE)

The little, plump periwinkles of Great Britain home in on bladder wrack, a type of seaweed trimmed with rounded green bumps, and feed there. Although the bright-yellow and dark-brown Flat Winkles *(Littorina littoralis)* stand out from the wrack, the green individuals blend in with almost perfect camouflage.

Americans rarely eat the larger winkles *(Littorina littorea)*, but Europeans do, and some pubs still place these boiled sea snails on the bar as a dunk-it-yourself snack with sauce and utensils called winkle pins on the side. Based on the evidence in prehistoric middens, the tradition of eating periwinkles goes back a long time.

The knobbed and striated Common Prickly Winkle *(Nodilittorina tuberculata)*, the more formal Beaded Periwinkle *(Tectarius muricatus)*, and the spotted Dwarf Brown Periwinkle *(Littorina mespillum)* are a few of the prettiest of this relatively undistinguished family.

PERIWINKLES AND BLACK TURBan Snails *(Tegula funebralis)*, left, share the same rocky habitat off the coast of Oregon. In Florida, these Zebra Periwinkles *(Littorina ziczac)* also favor rocky crevices between the two tide lines.

SUNDIALS
(ARCHITECTONICIDAE)

A pinwheel in slow motion comes close to describing the pattern superimposed on the Common American Sundial's (*Architectonica nobilis*) regular whorls. The well-balanced spiral design incorporates alternating brown-and-white checked lines, thinner brown lines, and subtle white beaded lines. Also known as the Architecture Shell, it does appear to have come from the careful rendering of a skilled draftsman's pen. Many of the approximately forty tropical species look flat compared to most shells.

The smaller, plainer Keeled Sundial (*Architectonica peracuta*) is less than 1 inch (2.5 cm) at adulthood; prices for this uncommon shell hover around fifty dollars for a perfect specimen, proof that not only showy shells command high prices.

THIS PACIFIC SUNDIAL *(ARCHI-tectonica maxima)* (left) closely resembles its common American cousin, both of which range over large areas. In the United States, the Common American Sundial lives in sandy, shallow-bottom water from North Carolina southward and from Baja, California southward.

THE VIOLET SEA SNAIL HAS many aliases throughout the world. It and other members of the Janthina family, unlike most other shells, spend all or part of their lives adrift in the open ocean.

PURPLE SNAILS
(JANTHINIDAE)

The ancient, predominantly white Hebrew prayer shawl had just four blue threads hanging from its corners. This tradition most likely was influenced by the rarity of the blue dye from the snail *Janthina janthina,* which in ancient times was a hard-to-procure, much-revered substance. The useful secretions of the Purple Snail took on a sociological importance similar to that of purple Murex dye (see page 70).

The Purple, or Violet, Snail is an interesting subject in and of itself. Its delicate-looking pale lavender shell camouflages the animal against the purply blues of sea and sky, hiding it from avian predators above and piscine predators below.

Found throughout the warmer waters of the world, *J. janthina* builds a raft of mucous air bubbles atop its shell and sails along the ocean's surface, drifting with the currents—notably the Gulf Stream along the United States. The animals are, to some extent, at the mercy of the winds and can suffer from mass strandings. As noted in *The Audubon Society Field Guide to North American Seashells,* in 1897 malacologist Charles T. Simpson came upon a number of Purple Snails: "As far as the eye could see, [the beach] was a mass of the most intense color... from below low water to the highest tide mark they were piled up... over shoe-top deep." The snails do not live long in the colder waters outside the Gulf Stream, and as they travel north into the cold, some wash up along the shores of Cape Cod.

WENTLETRAPS

(EPITONIIDAE)

The rose-tinted and alabaster Precious Wentletrap *(Epitonium scalare)* provides a good illustration of the fickleness of supply and demand. From 1700 on, the Precious Wentletrap was a rarity that captivated collectors and brought in several hundred dollars per shell. Stories abound of rice paste counterfeits being manufactured in China. The only way that a collector could tell the two apart was to submerge both in water; the replica would dissolve. In the twentieth century came more specimens uncovered in the waters between eastern Asia and Australia. Today, sophisticated trawling and diving have made the shell an affordable collectible, though it is still considered relatively uncommon. The irony is that if a forgery came to light now—none are documented—the rice paste facsimile would be worth much more than the shells, currently worth about thirty dollars.

The wentletrap species names hint at their rank within the world of shell connoisseurs. The stunning white, almost angelically pure Noble Wentletrap *(Sthenorytis pernobilis)* represents this interesting family in Florida and the Caribbean, while the more staid Magnificent Wentletrap *(Epitonium magnificum)* comes from the depths off of Japan. Malacologists and collectors look to the waters from Texas to Panama for a living example of Mitchell's Wentletrap *(Amaea mitchelli),* a beautiful brown-and-white shell that eludes all but a few dredgers.

One look at the family reveals why conchologists borrowed the German word *Wendeltrappe* or the Dutch *wenteltrappe*—which means "spiral staircase"—to describe the shells. The sophisticated, highly sculpted shells exhibit an unusual, pronounced ribbing that crosses the convex whorls.

THE PRECIOUS WENTLETRAP BE-longs to a large family that includes a number of unusual sea-anemone eaters. The family also gives rise to an extraordinary number of sinistral shells.

SLIPPER OR CUP-AND-SAUCER SHELLS
(CREPIDULIDAE)

An intriguing strategy developed among the Atlantic Slipper Shells *(Crepidula fornicata),* which plant themselves in one place to feed and grow. They attach themselves to other mollusks—scallops or mussels, for example—and gradually sculpt themselves to the shape of their host. This seemingly innocuous behavior can become a problem when the host is a commercial species such as the oyster. Slipper shells, for instance, were accidentally introduced to the waters off the English coast by a shipwreck. They invaded the local oyster beds and thrived, threatening their bivalve cousins. Regular dredging now keeps the problem in check.

Half of the approximately sixty species of Crepidulidae occur in North America. Not particularly prized by collectors, the slipper or cup-and-saucer shells make interesting beginner specimens because of the small shelf or cup visible on the shell's underside. Most scientists agree that in the absence of an operculum, the shelf acts as a protective device.

CARRIER SHELLS
(XENOPHORIDAE)

The carrier shells, too, carve out a unique niche for themselves among sea creatures. Rather than growing on top of another shell, they acquire shells, pebbles, and ocean litter to place on their own shells. Why they do it remains a mystery, although one possible explanation is camouflage. This endearing habit has given rise to a few nicknames: The Robust Carrier *(Xenophora robusta)* is called the "original shell collector," carriers that pick up shells are aptly dubbed "conchologists," and pebble picker-uppers are "geologists."

DUBBED THE QUARTERDECK and the Boat Shell, the Atlantic Slipper Shell sometimes lives on other shells, taking on their shape. All have the shelf that gives the family its common name.

TO AN UNFAMILIAR EYE, THE
Japanese Carrier Shell looks
more like a man-made three-
dimensional collage than a
natural creation by
Xenophora pallidula.

TRUE OR WINGED CONCHS
(STROMBIDAE)

The Greeks coined the word *konche*, but the term signified bivalves, not gastropods, and certainly not Strombidae. As time passed the definition expanded to include any large bivalve or univalve. By the sixteenth century *conch* meant a large marine gastropod. Some folks today still call any big, pretty seashell with a large body whorl and conical spire a conch. However the Swedish scientist Linnaeus attached the name to these "true" conchs, classified together because they all have a notch on the lower outer lip. Common usage also spilled over into the family of Melongenidae, or Crown Conchs (see page 79). True Conchs (also known as Winged Conchs), Spider Conchs, Tibia Shells (also known as Shinbone Strombs), and the single-species *Terebellum* genus comprise the Strombidae family.

The first conch to travel to Europe may have accompanied Christopher Columbus. Once on the Continent, the shell caught on as a graceful oddity of the natural world. The Victorians displayed their conch shells as art or incorporated them into gardens, fountains, and grottoes.

In anthropological guise, conchs—like tritons and helmet shells—acted as trumpets all over the world, from Mexico to Tonga and even in the United States among Hopi Indians. For some, the shell was just a shell; others saw it as a fundamental symbol. For instance, according to anthropologist Jane Safer, "In Chinese folklore the spirit who lives within the conch shell controls weather and protects against the sea's dangers...." Much of its folklore parallels that of the helmets and tritons (see pages 66 and 69).

THE FLORIDA FIGHTING CONCH (right) grows to between 2¾ and 4½ inches (6 and 11 cm) high—petite compared to the conchs that measure in at a foot (30 cm) tall. A good beginner's beach shell, the conch can often be found on the sand bars of western Florida.

CONCHS (ABOVE) INHABIT
shallow waters that receive
lots of sunlight, a combination
that encourages growth of sea
grass and symbiotic algae,
the conchs' primary food
sources.

IMMATURE CONCHS LOOK nothing like their adult counterparts; they lack the great lip and more closely resemble an offbeat form of cone shell than a conch. As adults, all true warm water Strombus conchs have a notch on their lower outer lip; the small indentation looks as if someone pinched off a bit of shell.

More than seventy conch species inhabit the world's warmer waters, and only four of these live off the mainland United States, primarily off the coast of southern Florida. Yet the reputation of these shells precedes them. Most people who have even a passing interest in shells have probably admired a large *Strombus* conch (up to 1 foot [30.5 cm] high), in a souvenir stand if not on the beach. The famed—and tasty—cracked conch of the Caribbean is more than likely the Pink Conch *(Strombus gigas),* whose lovely pink interior occasionally produces pink pearls. The shell differs substantially when immature. The young "rollers," as they are called, lack the dramatically extended lip.

The dark parietal wall of the Florida Fighting Conch *(Strombus alatus),* which is sometimes a ruddy burnt red, may bring to mind the flush of a scrapper after a tussle. This conch's name probably comes from the family's digitlike operculum, which strikes out against predators when provoked. (By working as a lever, it also helps move the animal forward.) Collectors tend to seek out the purple-and-white lined, 4- to 6-inch (10.2- to 15.2-cm) mottled brown Rooster-Tailed Conchs *(Strombus gallus)* of the Caribbean and the rare Goliath Conch—with its huge, flaring outer lip—that can reach heights of 15 inches (38.1 cm).

THE CARIBBEAN HAWK-WING Conch *(Strombus raninus),* which grows to four inches (10 cm) high, has a dwarf cousin found only around Lake Worth, Florida.

Farther afield lie the breeding grounds of the more elaborate "horned" Bull Conch *(Strombus taurus)* and the descriptively named Laciniated (fringed) Conch *(Strombus sinuatus),* both from the Pacific Ocean and both deserving of a cherished place in a collection.

The nine or ten species of striking—and sought-after—*Lambis* conchs look like plainer members of the family Strombidae, except that they have long, spinelike protuberances that jut out from the outer lip. They look as if the shells alone, without the help of the animal inside, could get up and walk away—and sting if necessary. Connoisseurs are drawn to the delicate lavender-and-yellow color scheme of the rare Violet Spider Conch *(Lambis violacea)* of Mauritius; the slender-spined Pilsbry's Spider Conch; and the False Scorpion Conch *(Lambis robusta).* The Giant Spider Conch *(Lambis truncata)* is not as rare—but it has the rare quality, some believe, of being an aphrodisiac.

The extraordinary Spindle, or Shinbone, Tibia *(Tibia fusus)* is one of the great showpieces of the shell world. Its creamy white-and-orange outer lip extends into an almost needlelike siphonal appendage that epitomizes conchological grace. Although the shell hails from the Pacific, its colors call to mind the red canyon lands of Utah and the southwestern United States.

NEAR RELATIVES OF THE TRUE conchs, spider conchs live in the Indo-Pacific province of waters. Their collectible appeal dates back at least to the 1600s when one unmistakable spider conch appeared in a European portrait from 1645. Although many Arthritic Spider Conchs *(Lambis arthritica)* are shown here piled up, scholars classify the 6-inch (15-cm) shells as "uncommon." The slightly smaller Common Spider Conch *(Lambis lambis),* in silhouette, is considered an "abundant" species.

SHELLS AS MONEY

No one knows when shells first made the transition from objets d'art to currency, but some scholars date the earliest use of shell money to 2000 B.C. in ancient China. The tradition continued to Marco Polo's day and a bit beyond, even though minted coins then dominated the economy. While Polo was in China during the thirteenth century, the great adventurer recorded that the peasants of southwestern China paid their taxes with shells.

In the African nation of Dahomey, one local chieftain also requested shell payment for taxes after discovering counterfeit coins in the treasury. Shell money was not always used for tax payments, but paid for a variety of things. In North America, wampum bought necessities, from food to fare on the Brooklyn ferry, up until the mid-1800s. But perhaps the most notorious shell money stemmed from the cowrie exchanges in Africa that eventually fueled the slave trade.

Cowrie shells first traveled to West Africa via the Indian Ocean, primarily as ballast in Arabian merchant ships. The ships landed in North Africa, from whence the shells were then transported across the Sahara; later on, they were carried by European trading companies to Lisbon, Amsterdam, and London, and then to the West African coast. The shells even found their way to North America.

Arab and European seafarers found the royal monarchy of the Maldive Islands good trading partners. For rice and salt, the islanders gave the sea captains cowrie shells, which bought gold and slaves in Africa. Small, uniform, and durable, the Money Cowrie *(Cypraea moneta)* and the closely related Gold-Ring Cowrie *(Cypraea annulus)* were ideal for use as money because they were difficult to counterfeit. For a long time the royal family of the Maldives limited the flow of these shells into the world economy. Colonial influences, the end of the slave trade, and market flooding from enterprising Westerners collapsed the shell trade, which in its heydey extended over much of Africa and well into India.

Archaeologists have uncovered cowrie shells the world over: in the earliest graves in Egypt, at prehistoric cemeteries in the Caucasus Mountains, at archaeological sites in India dating from the first century A.D., and in Saxon women's graves in England. Even if all these shells were not accepted as money, they were exploited as status symbols and adornments. Far from their native shores they help anthropologists confirm the existence of trading routes.

Five Pacific Money Cowries were discovered in one of the aboriginal graves of the Roden Mounds along the Tennessee River in Alabama. Evidence suggests that they were brought to the Americas on one of Columbus's ships or by early Spanish explorers. The cowries were also used by the Hudson's Bay Company for bartering with the Cree and other Indians. In 1805, the Lewis and Clark expedition brought back a Native American dress decorated with some four dozen Money Cowries. Another Money Cowrie was unearthed near the Onatonabee Serpent Mound in Ontario, Canada. In both cases, investigators believed that the shells came from the Hudson's Bay Company's stock.

That Native Americans would be attracted to the shiny Money Cowries makes sense, since they employed shell money from their own coasts. The use of wampum, predominantly made from different species of quahogs, spread from the Native Americans to the early white settlers. In addition to its buying power, wampum served a ceremonial purpose: Tribes living along the Atlantic coast from New England to Virginia made wampum—which was also used for ornaments—to record treaties and transactions between different Indian nations. Black wampum, fashioned from the small purple section of the Hard-Shelled Clam, or Northern Quahog *(Merceneria merceneria),* proved more valuable than the white wampum, which was made from the white part of the quahog or from the central column of the common Busycon whelk. In the early 1800s, the United States government outlawed wampum because of the prevalence of counterfeit currency in the young nation.

Northwestern Native Americans had access to tusk shells—long, slender shells that lent themselves to being strung as necklaces. These *Dentalium* shells paid for ritual debts and served as cash in more common transactions. For instance, anthropologist Jane Safer learned that among the Yurok Indians of California, ten twelve-shell strings of tusk shells made a dowry for a wealthy family. Five strings paid a fine for adultery, while three strings bought a house.

COWRIES

(CYPRAEIDAE)

No one can say for sure which shells attract the most collectors, but cowries—small, multicolored, smooth, beanlike shells—seduce and enchant as powerfully as a siren song; the only difference, perhaps, is that the cowries' admirers live to tell of their seducers' beauty and of their extraordinary ability to excite a passion for shell collecting. Cowries have a sensuality and a sensibility all their own. Man has created legends around them, conferring upon them a status that few other shells have acquired.

From a simple perspective, the Mayans used cowrie shells to indicate zero. Yet within many cultures around the world the cowrie has stood for all mankind; for womankind; for authority, royalty, and privilege; for eyes; for the skeleton; and for disease.

In a small way the cowrie illustrates the concept of syncretism: believing in two contradictory ideas at once. The Yoruba of Nigeria identify cowrie shells with their god Obatala, who created man. Obatala also has a close association with the color white, which the Yoruba observed in many cowries, reminding them of smallpox pustules; to counteract the association, the shells were dyed blue for luck. Thus the same object that represented something bad, with transformation could also represent something good.

Among the Bambara people of Mali cowries symbolized humanity. The Bambara decorated wooden masks with Ring Cowries *(Cypraea annulus)* and Money Cowries *(Cypraea moneta)* to wear during the meetings of a secret society.

East Indians have worn Money Cowries on headdresses to protect vulnerable children and animals from the evil eye. This association with the eye extends all the way to Europe. The connection makes sense because a cowrie can look like an eye with a bit of a stretch; by extension, it makes sense that within a magical system the cowrie would hold power to defend against the evil eye.

Cowries also appeared on headdresses of the Kalash people in Afghanistan; complemented by a woolen pompom, the shell-adorned article is a sign of betrothal. Not too far away, in Ethiopia, the Galla people related Ring Cowries and femaleness; thus women wore leather belts strung with cowries and dove shells.

ENTHUSIASTIC SHELLERS ARE NO less avid than ornithologists or stamp collectors and frequently plan vacations around shelling hot spots such as the Philippines and Fiji, where collectors go in search of the great Golden Cowrie.

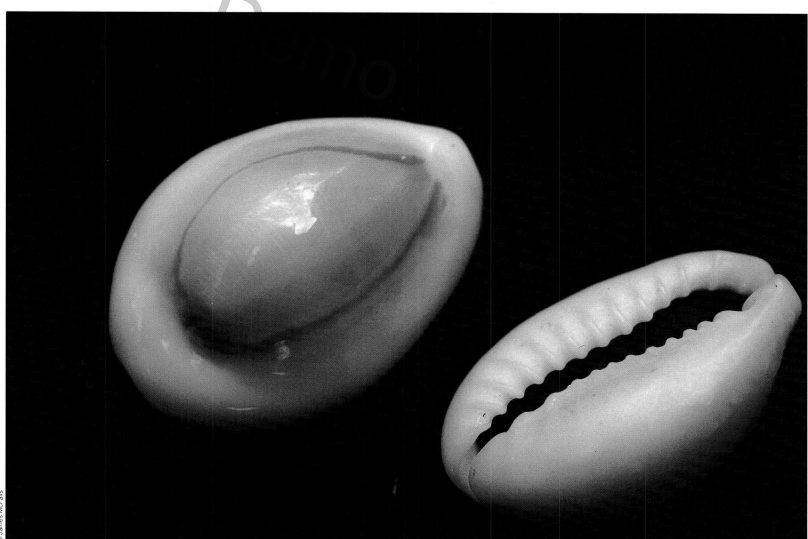

RING COWRIES (ABOVE), ALSO
known as Gold-ringed Cow-
ries, were once valued almost
as much as Money Cowries.
Malacologist R. Tucker Abbott
estimated that people have
collected more than a thousand pounds of these two
shells over the ages.

THE COWRIE'S MANTLE PRO-
tects the shell, leaving it un-
marred for collectors attracted
by the shell's characteristic
gloss. Indo-Pacific Tiger Cowries have turned up in a
prehistoric pit-dwelling in England, a historic fact that can
enhance the shell's value.

Cowries also denote authority in places as varied as Zaire (among the Kuba people), Taiwan (among the Paiwan people), and Fiji (where the celebrated Golden Cowrie, *Cypraea aurantium*, stands for royalty). If a king in Fiji wears a Golden Cowrie, he gives it cultural worth; it then becomes taboo for commoners. Fijians also believe that the cowrie shell receives the soul of a person who has died.

Practically, cowries have a few uses, too. Octopuses find cowries tasty tidbits, so in Tahiti the Tiger Cowrie *(Cypraea tigris)*, Reticulated Cowrie *(Cypraea maculifera)*, and Ventriculate Cowrie *(Cypraea ventriculus)* make good bait for the tentacled creatures. In addition, Mindanaoans in the Philippines polished hemp with the Tiger Cowrie.

Cowries even found a place in what was to become the United States. When French fur traders exchanged goods with the Indians, cowries exchanged hands as well; the trappers are credited with introducing the shells to North America. The well-liked cowries quickly became indications of wealth and often accompanied their owners to the grave.

Of the 190 species of cowries, 6 inhabit Caribbean waters and only 1 frequents the coast of California. Roughly translated, the genus name *Cypraea* means "shell of the Cyprian goddess"; Aphrodite, the goddess in question, supposedly rose from the ocean foam very near Cyprus.

Fortunately for collectors many beautiful cowries are relatively common in the Indo-Pacific. Rarities include the speckled Cox's Cowrie *(C. coxeni)*; the intriguingly blotched Map Cowrie *(C. mappa)*, whose slight greenish tint gives rise to its common name; the Stolid Cowrie *(C. stolida)* with its palominolike markings; and the very unusual Leucodon Cowrie *(C. leucodon)*. If no new finds are uncovered by the time this book goes to press, only seven specimens of the Prince Cowrie have surfaced. More intriguing, however, are the shells from deep-water species that only materialize in the stomachs of predatory fish. Fulton's Cowrie *(C. fultoni)* and the Great Spotted Cowrie are two examples of these exceptionally rare specimens.

The more common, pretty Eyed Cowrie *(C. argus)*, with its distinct open-and-filled rings pattern, played a part in our linguistic history. As the Eyed Cowries traveled from the Indo-Pacific to Italy, the sailors thought they saw a resemblance between the shell and a piglet, so they invented the nickname *porcellino*, which means " piglet." The word passed north to France where it became—and remains—*porcelaine*, the term for the cowrie. *Porcelaine* evolved further when someone recognized the similarities between the sheen of the shell and that of glazed china, a new import to France at the time. The dishes acquired the name *porcelaine* also, and although we've lost the association with the cowrie, we still call fine china porcelain. The oval-shaped, toothy cowrie has the smoothness of porcelain because its mantle covers and protects the shell.

EGG SHELLS
(OVULIDAE)

When stood on end the milky egg shells look almost like birds readying themselves for the night, their heads folded into their breasts. Among the Manus people of the Admiralty Islands the Great Egg Cowry *(Ovula ovum)* intimates that the one who wears it comes from a noble family. The relatively large shell, which grows up to 5 inches (12.7 cm), may sit on the prow of a canoe, attracting attention much as the winged figure on the hood of a Rolls Royce does. The Manus include the shell in belts, hang it from their houses, and wear it during battle and in war dances.

In parts of New Guinea, warriors incorporated two egg shells into a fiber neckpiece that they could hold between their teeth in battle. Their version of special effects, the large egg shells, with smaller nassa shells between them, gave the warriors a broadened grimace of sorts, making them look fiercer to the enemy.

The Shuttlecock, or Shuttle, Shell *(Volva volva)* is quite different. On either side of the main shell body, slender siphonlike spikes extend outward to form a "grin" not unlike Jack Nicholson's as the Joker in *Batman*.

A SENSE OF WHIMSY AND HU-mor motivated someone to name *Ovula ovum* the Poached Egg Cowrie. In this case both the common name and the scientific name refer to the shell's egglike shape.

MOON SHELLS
(NATICIDAE)

Endowed with an unusually large foot, a moon snail can envelop most of its shell. The snail's evolution shows a trend toward a smaller shell and larger foot. The adaptation aids the animal's carnivorous habits well, for it is a very successful hunter of the marine world, feasting on as many as six or seven clams each day. The moon snail's radular teeth saw into a clam, and, in some species, an acid secreted through the snail's proboscis makes quicker work of the task.

Found the world over, the moon snail's habitats vary from the intertidal zone to great depths. The Butterfly Moon *(Naticarius alapapilionis* or *Natica alapapilionis)* from the Indo-Pacific is one of the prettiest species, with dark-and-light checked striations banding around the shell. The orblike shell shape—which inspired the common name—contributes to its appeal; so does the buttonlike top on species such as the Shark Eye *(Neverita duplicata* or *Polinices duplicatus)* of the East Coast and, to a lesser extent, the pretty Colorful Atlantic Natica *(Natica canrena).* On a good specimen, the latter's swirls could double for a raspberry or chocolate coulis in a custard sauce at a fine restaurant.

A SHARK EYE (LEFT) TAKES ITS name from the pattern of dark and light whorls on the shell, which gives it the appearance of an eye. These shells are quite common on sandy shores from Massachusetts to Florida.

SHARK EYES, THE GOLDEN Moon *(Polinices aurantius)* (below), and many other moon snails create an unusual egg sac—made of sand grains and snail mucus—that often washes ashore.

HELMET SHELLS

(CASSIDAE)

Prized in days past because craftsmen turned the larger shells into delicate cameos, the helmet shells' layers alternate between brown and white. Most shells share this stratified structure; the helmet shells—and similarly constructed conchs—are simply thicker than most other shells and can withstand the carving without breaking.

Many cultures, such as those on coral islands, adapted to using shells—especially strong, thick shells like the helmets—as raw material for tools and utensils when resources such as metal, stone, and clay were lacking. From Africa to New Guinea to the New World, man has modified helmet shells to create bowls as well as ladles, adzes as well as scrapers. And when the Red Helmet Shell *(Cypraecassis rufa)* turned up in a Cro-Magnon grave in France, the species helped archaeologists trace ancient trade routes.

The King *(Cassis tuberosa)* and Queen *(Cassis madagascarien-sis)* helmets (also known, confusingly, as King and Queen conchs) have a terrifying beauty. Their fierce, toothy, over-stretched "grins" transform the shells into monsters of the deep. And yet, the fleshy "lips" and white "teeth" lend vigor and majesty to these shells, so much so that primitive peoples attributed great power to the shells.

Uncommon and attractive specimens include the pale Royal Bonnet *(Sconsia striata)* and Dennison's Morum *(Morum dennisoni)*, both of the West Indies, and the pink-embellished Exquisite Morum *(Morum exquisitum)*.

The brownish-red rectangular markings on the Checkerboard Helmet *(Phalium areola)* are interesting enough, but the animal that produces the striking shell also fabricates a fascinating liquid. The secretion paralyzes sea urchins, the snail's primary food, and the helpless prey then sheds its protective spines, leaving it exposed to its predator.

THE RED HELMET SHELL ALSO goes by the name Bull or Bull's Mouth Helmet, and its most notable asset is reflected in its rosy name. The approximately 6-inch (15-cm) shell lends itself to orange-hued, detailed cameo work.

A FULL LIFE FOR A TRITON'S
Trumpet (above) typically
spans six years. It and its Caribbean kin differ only slightly.
The Indo-Pacific species tend
to have more space between
the teeth on the outer lip.

TRITONS

(CYMATIIDAE)

Edith Hamilton, the doyenne of classical mythology, states simply that "Triton was the trumpeter of the sea. His trumpet was a great shell." That great shell now goes by the name Triton's Trumpet—whether it is recognized as *Cymatium tritonis, Charonia tritonis,* or *Triton tritonis.* Other triton shells performed as trumpets around the world—Neolithic people of the Mediterranean, Shinto priests in Japan, Hawaiians, and island folk of the Indo-Pacific all blew on the shell as a great horn. Peter Paul Rubens even depicted the blowing of tritons in a painting detailing the arrival of Maria de Medici in France.

The call of the shell gathered worshipers, warriors, and welcomers; it accompanied drinkers and mourners; and it kept evil spirits at bay. The shell's importance influenced ancient minters: Figures sounding a triton shell appear on Sicilian coins that circulated more than two thousand years ago, and on clay seals from Crete that could be twice as old. A more recent representation can be seen alongside Atlantic Murexes in Barcelona at the cathedral built by the eccentric architect Antonio Gaudi.

The largest tritons reach lengths of 15 or 16 inches (38.1 or 40.6 cm) at maturity. In many instances their surface designs match the marbled swirls of hand-dyed Italian paper. Pretty teeth along the inner or outer lips complement the natural patterns.

Although only a dozen or so trumpet species exist—in the Caribbean and Indo-Pacific—more than a hundred species of hairy tritons inhabit the reefs and grassy flats of the world's waters. These odd but aptly named creatures produce a hairy covering on the outside of their shells that is unlike the smooth and sometimes transparent periostracum (outer covering) on most other shells.

A HAIRY PERIOSTRACUM, OR covering, normally cloaks this hairy triton *(Cymatium rubecula)* (below) of New Guinea. In the United States, the family is represented by the Atlantic or Common Hairy Triton *(Cymatium pileare),* an inhabitant of both the Atlantic and Pacific coasts.

MUREX SHELLS
(MURICIDAE)

The rich purple mentioned in Lord Byron's poem reflected the attitude that many ancient Mediterranean peoples had toward the extraordinary purple-red dyed cloth that originated in Phoenicia. This cloth, like the gold that complemented it, deserved admiration. Only those with wealth or power could afford to buy and wear articles dyed with what is now called Royal Tyrian Purple.

The people of Tyre and Sidon perfected a dying process using the glandular secretions from two marine gastropods: the Dye Murex *(Murex brandaris)* and the related rock shell *Thais haemastoma.* To produce just over ½ ounce (14 g) of dye, the Phoenicians used approximately 12,000 snails. So about 400,000 individual animals were needed to color 50 pounds (19 kg) of wool. Of necessity, the Phoenicians spread out far and wide looking for new snail beds to supply their dye works.

Such extravagance put a premium on the dye. In ancient times Babylonians, who used the dye before the Phoenicians, dressed their idols in the purple cloth. The high priest of Israel wore robes of Murex purple. In Greece and Rome, donning robes of Tyrian purple indicated status; great artists and orators wore the color, as did Julius and Augustus Caesar. Nero, too, wore Tyrian purple and forbade anyone else from doing so; to disregard his decree meant death.

The dye's qualities helped to establish its reputation. The brilliance lasted for many years, and beyond that, the color stayed long after the brilliance disappeared. One story relates that Alexander the Great, as a result of his conquests, took possession of more than 5,000 pounds (1865 kg) of the cloth that had been in storage for 180 years. Time had not dimmed the color. Some of the purple-dyed cloth exists to this day in the form of mummy wrappings.

THE MUREX FAMILY CAN BE DIvided into two rough categories: those shells with spines and those without. The Snipe's Bill, or Snipe's Head, Murex *(Murex haustellum)* (left)—a huskier, unspined version of the Venus Comb Murex— (right) exemplifies the latter.

The Assyrian came down like the wolf on the fold,

And his cohorts were gleaming in purple and gold

Lord Byron

"Destruction of Sennacherib"

But the family of Murex snails yields more than dye. These gastropods produce some of the loveliest shells in the molluscan world. What looks like a long backbone with slender spines extending outward from it characterizes the well-known Venus Comb Murex *(Murex pecten,* formerly *Murex triremus).* This lovely shell with all its spines intact commands much attention from collectors. It is the same shell that more than one artist has depicted as a mermaid's comb, capturing its fantastic appeal.

An aura of fantasy surrounds this family. Other Murex shells appear to move and writhe; their lacy, outstretched shelly arms dance outside the water. The simple frills, knobs, and protrusions become wings or scorpion legs, coral figurines, even leafy vegetables and eccentric funghi in the eyes of enchanted observers.

Collectors head for the popular Rose-Branch Murex *(Murex palmarosae),* the bony-looking Clavus Murex *(Murex elongatus),* the webbed Beau's Murex *(Murex beaui),* and the orange-and-white Cabrit's Murex *(Murex cabriti).* Although many of the more than seven hundred species of Murex are common, more often than not the individuals gathered are not in perfect condition.

In Mexico, the Huichol people regarded the Blackened Murex *(Murex nigritus)* as a signal to the gods. They sounded the sonorous shell horn during the tamale feasts of the corn harvests. The Blackened Murex is an unusual shell primarily because, when it is immature, the shell is almost all white; as it ages, it becomes flecked with black until black takes over as the dominant color.

ROUGHLY 140 SPECIES OF Murex shells occur within range of the United States. Most of these frequent the waters off the Carolina shore, south of it, and California south. This pile-up, however, was photographed on Reeds Beach in New Jersey.

BECAUSE MUREX SHELLS IN PERfect condition are hard to come by—and also because some species are confusingly similar—the family has not caught on with beginning collectors even though the shells are among the most striking. Here are beautiful, though not perfect, examples of the Pinkmouthed Murex *(Murex* or *Phyllonotus erythrostomus)* (above) and the Snipe's Bill or Snipe's Head Murex *(Murex naustellum)* (right).

RANGING WIDELY FROM THE Arctic to the tropics, whelks such as the Neptune Whelk (below) become familiar to shellers who walk the beaches of both American coasts.

WHELKS
(BUCCINIDAE)

Although whelks don't have the flash-and-dazzle appeal of cone, olive, and murex shells, this large family interests naturalists because they live in such varied environments, from the Arctic to the tropics to the Antarctic. The buccinids' vertical range varies as widely as their geographic range. The abyssal depths, which malacologist R. Tucker Abbott defines as "water over 5,000 feet (1,500 m) in depth," yields whelks, as do low-tide or intertidal areas off practically all the American coasts.

Whelks, and their cousins in the Melongenidae family, make infrequent appearances on the dining table: They've been found in middens and fished commercially in recent times. One species, the Common Northern Whelk *(Buccinum undatum),* or Waved Whelk, didn't make it to the table; instead it readied sailors for their feasts. Some clever seaman discovered that the leathery clusters of whelk egg capsules made good washcloths; perhaps he was the one who nicknamed them "sea wash balls."

The Neptunes—there's one in New England *(Neptunea lyrata decemcostata)* and one in the Northwest *(Neptunea lyrata)*—stand out among the North American species because of the decidedly spiraled ridges on most specimens. In contrast, the White-Spotted Engina *(Engina turbinella),* or Spotted Lesser Whelk, is smaller (¼ to ⅝ inch or .6 to 1.6 cm) and more top-shaped, with white knobs set against a dark-brown background. The white beaded, latticed surface of Cande's Beaded Phos *(Antillophos candei)* is, again, very different from most other members of the family and brings to mind the texture of a white-on-white chenille bedspread.

SOME SPECIES OF *BUCCINIDAE* whelks and some fulgur whelks of the family *Melongenidae* appear to be very similar (above). Collectors sometimes take up scuba diving to get a closer look at such activities as whelks laying their eggs or enveloping their prey.

LEFT-HANDED OR RIGHT-HANDED?

The concept of a gastropod shell being right- or left-handed can be difficult to grasp by newcomers to malacology. To understand this idea it helps to be familiar with a few terms—*apex* and *spire* in particular. The only problem is that most shell glossaries seem to be as spirally oriented as some of the shells they are defining. For instance, many texts define the apex as "the tip of the spire." The spire means "all whorls above the body whorl." The body whorl definition for gastropods actually begins to make sense to a neophyte: "the final whorl" or "the last and largest whorl," the whorl that "contains most of the animal's soft parts." So go back to our initial attempt to identify the difference between a dextrally or right-handed coiling shell; hold the shell in question with the apex up and the opening, or aperture, facing you, and look to see if the spiral is clockwise or counterclockwise.

When held as described, most shells coil dextrally (clockwise down the spire), with a few exceptions such as the Lightning and Perverse whelks and a number of margin shells. When a sinistrally (counterclockwise) coiling shell appears, such as a left-handed chank or cone, it becomes a much-sought-after curiosity.

Malacologist S. Peter Dance reported in the mid-1970s that within 16 families, "perhaps no more than 75 species have been found with reversed shells."

CROWN CONCHS

(MELONGENIDAE)

The normally left-handed or sinistral Lightning Whelk *(Busycon contrarium)* and Perverse Whelk *(Busycon perversum)* reverse the standard in the shell world; the rare specimens are those that grow dextrally (see page 78).

The Perverse Whelk inhabits the waters off the Gulf Coast of Florida, yet archaeologists excavating at sites as far inland as Arkansas have found shell dippers used as eating utensils dating from the Hopewell period (200 B.C. to A.D. 500), indicating that a trade route was probably firmly in place at the time. Closer to home, archaeologists in Florida uncovered a Perverse Whelk attached to a piece of wood that most likely functioned as a club head. Sturdier and heavier than the Lightning Whelk, it—or one of its near relatives—also performed as a horn for Chickasaw Indians during the time of DeSoto's explorations of the Sunshine State. Native Americans were also producing money strands or belts using *Busycon* whelks as white wampum when the first colonists arrived.

This family, of fulgur whelks and crown conchs, is well known along the coasts of the United States. The largest of the shells can reach up to 16 inches (40.6 cm), which helps to explain its usefulness to man. The connoisseur will appreciate the subtle colors, markings, and structure of the shells as well, especially those of the bold Florida Crown Conch *(Melongena corona)*, the pastel West Indian Crown Conch *(Melongena melongena)*, and the light-and-dark Lightning Whelk.

THE BANDED FLORIDA CROWN Conch reaches heights of 8 inches (20 cm); this scavenger feeds on dead fish and mollusks although it has also been known to attack live bivalves

NASSA SHELLS
(NASSARIIDAE)

The knobs and ribbings of many of these shells give the family one of its common names—basket whelk—as well as its family name. *Nassa* comes from the Latin for "wicker basket." Harder to imagine is how these relatively small shells (ranging from ¼ inch to 3 inches or .6 to 7.6 cm) acquired the common name *dog whelk*.

The Tolai of Melanesia threaded the shells into long strings called *tambu*, which could then be coiled into the shape of a large hoop. When stretched out the coiled strings might measure a mile or longer. *Tambu*, used for all sorts of purchases originally, at last look served as payment only for rituals: births, marriages, funerals.

In West Irian, New Guinea, an area that adventure travel companies have just recently opened up, the people weave nassa shells into a bark cloth mask so tightly that the shells appear to form a knitted chain. With "closed" cowrie shell eyes so as not to see—and harm—the living, the mask represents a dead person's spirit during his funeral.

Because the family is large—one estimate counts more than 350 species worldwide—and classification varies from author to author and thus from collector to collector, many of these pretty shells are overlooked by amateurs.

SPINDLE AND TULIP SHELLS
(FASCIOLARIIDAE)

Collectors fancy spindle shells, taking pleasure in the even, building whorls and graceful length reminiscent of old-fashioned Christmas tree ornaments. The Distaff Spindle *(Fusinus colus)* of the Indo-Pacific represents the family well with lovely dimpled hills and valleys sculpting the upper portion of the 4- to 7-inch (10.2- to 17.8-cm) shell.

Of about 30 species from around the United States, the Florida Horse Conch *(Pleuroplaca gigantea)* stands out as the largest member of the Fasciolariidae family—and its 23-inch-long (58.4-cm) body makes it the largest shell to be found off the American coasts. The smaller Banded Tulip *(Fasciolaria lilium)* brings to mind a calico or tabby cat; distinct dark-brown spiral lines stripe the overall pattern of white, gray, and brown or orange markings. Coue's Spindle Shell *(Fusinus couei)* manifests a different kind of beauty based on its even whiteness and sculpted spiral cords; it takes its name from its discoverer, a French ship's captain. The rarest collector's item on the European side of the Atlantic is the Closter Spindle *(Fusinus closter)*, whose body resembles a puffier version of the Distaff Spindle.

THE EXTRAORDINARY, ROSE-tinted Spindle Tibia or Shin-bone Tibia *(Tibia fusus)* (right) of the Pacific Ocean boasts a sometimes 5-inch (12½-cm) long needlelike projection, lending the shell a powerful delicacy. The projection is actually a shelly tube that covers and protects the animal's siphon.

A TAPESTRY OF COLORS MARK this grouping of Banded and True Tulip Shells (right) from Sanibel Island, Florida. The True Tulip *(Fasciolaria tulipa)* can grow to 9½ inches (24 cm), while the Banded Tulip extends to just over 4 inches (10 cm). Both inhabit sandy or muddy bottoms in relatively shallow water off the south-eastern American coast.

OLIVE SHELLS
(OLIVIDAE)

Mayans carved exaggerated faces in olive shells, while half-way across the world men on the Pacific island of New Hebrides (now Vanuatu) fashioned related shells into dance rattles. A similar practice of using olive shells as noise-makers appears in Mexico. In the seventh century people from the area around Oaxaca made Panamanian Tent Olives *(Oliva porphyria)* into "tinklers" to call for rain. The tinklers made sounds similar to that of rain pitter-pattering. Because precipitation comes in the spring, it doesn't take a leap of the imagination to understand why museum depictions of Xipe Totec show this god of spring wearing a low belt adorned with these shells. As for its name, the Panamanian Tent Olive exhibits striking tent-shaped patterns that look like row upon row of a child's pointy-peaked mountains.

Another olive family member, the Purple Dwarf Olive *(Olivella biplicata),* held special symbolic significance for native Americans in the southwestern United States as well. To the Pueblos, this oval-shaped shell tinged with browns and pale purplish grays became associated with their war gods. The American Museum of Natural History in New York has in its collection a miniature Zuni bow and shield each with an olive shell incorporated into the design; the Zuni also attached shells to other ritual objects such as their animal fetishes, most likely to lend them luck during the hunt.

THE TENT OLIVE (LEFT), LIKE ALL others in its family, lives in the sand. Its shell is not affected by the potentially scratchy substrate because the mantle covers and protects the olive shell's glossy surface.

The association turns from war to women in the Klamath River area of northern California, where women strung *Olivella biplicata* shells into a necklace to be worn as part of the ritual of a young girl's initiation into adulthood during her first menstruation. The slender necklace alternates the shells with one, two, or three seeds.

Central California peoples decorated clothing with the smaller San Pedro Dwarf Olive *(Olivella pedroana)* and the Purple Dwarf Olive, the latter of which also appeared on the West Coast as money—although the practice was negligible in contrast to the widespread use of cowries and wampum as a monetary medium.

In the mid-1700s conchologist Dezallier d'Argenville claimed that he could make out three Roman letters on a specimen of *Oliva sayana,* the Lettered Olive. No one since really believes that observers can actually see letters, but the markings are unique enough to attract many collectors.

Olive shells are especially glossy because while the animal is alive the snail's mantle covers the shell. Collectors fancy the shells' smooth, stretched-out egg shapes and their usually crisp markings and colors. For example, the tricolor olive *(Oliva tricolor)* flaunts blue and yellow among its colors, an atypical example of strong, opposing colors abutting each other on a shell.

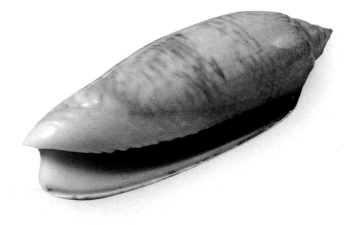

EXPERIENCED COLLECTORS know that low tide under the cover of a night sky is the best time to hunt olive shells (right). Fishermen have caught carnivorous Lettered Olives on crab-baited lures by accident. The Lettered Olives also feed on bivalve coquina shells.

MITER SHELLS
(MITRIDAE AND COSTELLARIIDAE)

The miters of the shell world crown a family of several hundred mollusks whose most famous members dwell in the shallow, warm waters from the coast of East Africa to Polynesia, with extraordinary concentrations in the Philippines.

Besides the resemblance of these shells to bishop's hats or Buddhist temple tops, the miter shell hides a winding, spiralling architectural pillar that malacologists call a columella. Although a columella appears in all coiled gastropods, miter shells, when sliced lengthwise, show a particularly exquisite screw-shaped columella.

With a comely shape, an extraordinary structure, and attractive colors of its own, the family also mimics other beauties of the shell world: olives, true conchs, and cones. Two are even named the Cone Miter *(Pterygia conus)* and the Olive-Shaped Miter *(Swainsonia olivaeformis)*.

The orange-spotted Episcopal Miter *(Mitra mitra)* is fairly common in Indo-Pacific waters, so it makes a good beginning collector's item. In North America, the Barbados Miter *(Mitra barbadensis)* found off southeastern Florida boasts a pretty reddish brown sheen.

THE EPISCOPAL MITER (BELOW and right) goes by another name: the Fusiform Miter, which describes its tapered shape. The Indo-Pacific shell haunts coral reefs in the Indo-Pacific and usually reaches heights of between 3 and 5 inches (7.5 and 12.5 cm).

CHANKS

(TURBINELLIDAE OR XANCIDAE)

With only about twenty-five species Turbinellidae is one of the smallest families of mollusks, yet man has revered them for centuries.

The Sacred Chank of India *(Turbinella pyrum)* is just that. Many depictions of the four-armed Hindu god Vishnu show him holding a left-handed chank, which represents either a weapon used to vanquish opponents or a musical instrument whose song announced victory over those enemies. The chank's association with Vishnu probably derives from a legend that, in short, holds that the devil hid a sacred text in the shell, and Vishnu rescued it. The chank shell's spiral structure probably also complements Vishnu's role as "the preserver of continuity."

According to anthropologist Jane Safer,

> It may well be that the Hindu priest serving medicine in the holy shell (the left-handed chank, usually decorated with gold and precious stones) to an ailing member of his community has found the strength of belief that gives him the power to produce a miracle. Seeing the shell's perfection in spite of its contrary conception, he is reminded of all the other wonders of creation and its greatness, and this mystical encouragement tends to give success to his performance.

Most Hindu peoples believe that anything from the sea is pure, which gives the shell added cultural value. Lacquered and cut into a bracelet, *Turbinella pyrum* is the equivalent of a wedding ring among some Hindu families. The bracelet signifies that the woman is married, and encourages good health and prosperity for her husband. She wears the charm until her husband dies, when she destroys it.

The women of the Burmese Lakher people wore chank shells as ornaments. These became heirlooms passed down from the groom's family to the female relatives of the bride.

In the Caribbean, the large size (8 to 10 inches or 20.3 to 25.4 cm) of a related shell, the Lamp Chank *(Xancus angulatus),* gave it a more practical use as a base for oil lamps.

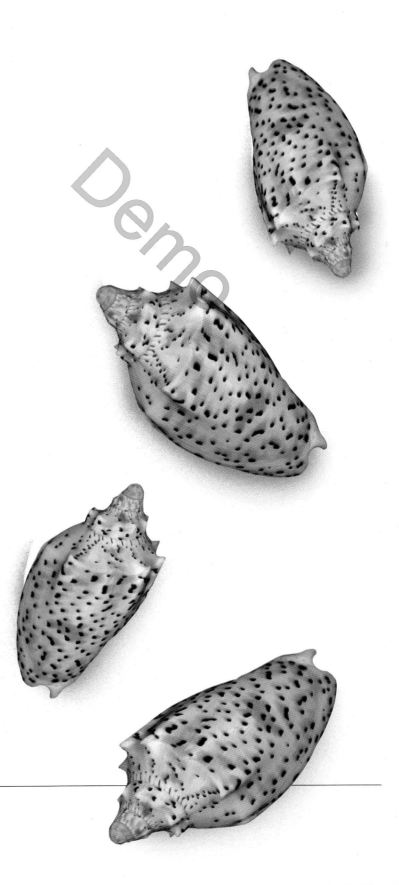

SILHOUETTES OF THE BAT VOlute of the Philippines (above) and an Australian volute barely do justice to this large and beautiful family that includes the "aristocrats of the shell world."

VOLUTES
(VOLUTIDAE)

Because of their striking markings and, in many cases, their larger size, many of the two hundred or so volute species attract collectors. In fact, these beauties are often called the aristocrats of the shell world.

A certain poetry rings from the species' names. The Music Volute *(Voluta musica)* of the Caribbean received its title because someone saw a resemblance between its markings—which can include five thin, dark bands and random spots—and the staff and notes of a musical score. The intricate patterns appear to each viewer in a different guise.

The Hebrew Volute *(Voluta ebraea)* provides another example of the shell equivalent of cloud-watching. One creative thinker drew parallels between its markings and the Hebrew alphabet. This handsome Brazilian species, which can grow to 5 inches (12.7 cm), boasts the zigzag patterns common to many volutes.

Whoever named the Junonia Volute *(Scaphella junonia)* likened its tawny brown spots to a peacock's eyes; the peacock, known as the "bird of Juno," lent its name inadvertently to the shell. Still a mystery to malacologists, Juno's Volute—as it is also called—lives in deep water, up to 250 feet (76 m) down. To find, rather than buy, a good specimen is considered a collector's feat.

Large Bailer—or Melon—shells, which are members of the volute family, reach lengths of 14 inches (35.6 cm) or more. The indigenous peoples of the tropical western Pacific used these to bail out their boats. The Ethiopian Volute *(Melo aethiopicus* or *Melo broderipi)* contributed to what anthropologists call the Kula ring, a trading circle of the Pacific in which ritual exchanges were as important as product exchanges. A necklace made from the Bailer and from clam shell disks could only be swapped for a bracelet made from *Conus leopardus,* the Leopard Cone shell. The formality of this agreed-upon exchange opened up negotiations for other less-well-defined bartering.

Rare species scattered throughout the world include the striking swag-covered Bednall's Volute *(Volutoconus bednalli)* and the brownish red streaked Lightning Volute *(Ericusa fulgetrum),* both of Australia; the Golden Volute *(Iredalina aurantina)* of New Zealand; the red-speckled *Cymbiola cymbiola* (the most recently collected specimen dates from the eighteenth century); the knobbed Festive Volute *(Festilyria festival),* which has commanded more than two thousand dollars at auction; the African "living fossil" *Volutocorbis abyssicola;* and a few others trawled from the great depths that some volutes are known to inhabit.

THIS MUSIC VOLUTE (BELOW) originated off the Caribbean island of Tobago, where the animal lived in water from 1 to 20 feet (30 cm to 6 m) deep. Most Music Volutes fall within a 1⅛- to 3¾-inch (2½- to 9-cm) size range.

SCIENTISTS KNOW VERY LITTLE about the 2½- to 5-inch (6- to 12-cm) Junonia shell (right) that lives in somewhat deep water off both coasts of Florida. Once considered very rare, it actually washes ashore more often than its spotted subfamily members, Kiener's Volute *(S. kieneri)* and Dohrn's Volute *(S. dohrni).*

MALACOLOGISTS ARE ALSO stumped when it comes to many specifics about nutmeg shells, especially those that inhabit the abyssal depths (to about 4500 feet [1350 m]). In contrast, some nutmegs, including the Common Nutmeg of the Atlantic coast, live from about the low tide line to approximately 50-foot (15-m) depths.

NUTMEGS
(CANCELLARIIDAE)

About 150 species make up this family of small (¼ to 3¼ inches or .6 to 8.3 cm), pretty, and eccentrically shaped shells. Many nutmegs have a squat, swollen, almost round or oval body whorl with a variety of relatively short, stepped spire whorls. Some spires appear scalloped, others have toothy edges, while still others resemble the spire whorls of helmet and spindle shells. Most are tropical or subtropical. The latticed Common Nutmeg *(Cancellaria reticulata)* surfaces quite frequently in shallow water off the eastern coast from the Carolinas to the Gulf Coast of Texas. Subspecies *C. reticulata adelae* (Adele's Nutmeg) makes rare appearances in the Florida Keys; it's smoother and paler than its more common cousin.

MARGIN SHELLS
(MARGINELLIDAE)

The beautifully tinted, glossy margin shells are also relatively small, with very low spires; most are between 1 and 3 inches (2.5 and 7.6 cm) at full growth, although some, such as the Teardrop Margin Shell *(Granulina ovuliformis),* only reach ⅛ inch (.3 cm) at maturity. Their general shape falls somewhere between that of cowrie shells (minus their teeth) and bubble shells. Several diagonal ridges on the bottom of the inner lip (the columella in this case) characterize the family, along with a thick edge—or margin—on the outer lip.

Margins are also noted for their high incidence of left-handed shells (see page 78); these account for as much as 40 percent of all known reversals, according to malacologist S. Peter Dance. Caribbean waters yield sinistral versions of the Common Atlantic Margin Shell *(Prunum apicinum* or *Marginella apicina),* which then sell for approximately twenty-five dollars, as opposed to one dollar or so for right-handed specimens.

The simplicity of the colorful Orange Marginella, or Orange Margin Shell *(Prunum carneum* or *Marginella carnea),* makes it a collectible if somewhat common West Indian species. The often overlooked beauty of this family, however, is the almost translucent white-spotted Frosted Margin Shell *(Prunum pruinosum* or *Marginella pruinosum).*

CONE SHELLS

(CONIDAE)

Just as Circe's beauty enticed Odysseus's men into danger, the glossy, beautifully patterned cone shell can lure shellers into hazardous situations. A few species can bring a man to his deathbed with just one sting. The alluring cones comprise only a single genus, *Conus,* that contains between four hundred and five hundred species—almost all of which are strikingly beautiful and very collectible. A high-gloss smoothness characterizes the cone-shaped shells, which hide a proboscis that, in turn, conceals harpoonlike stinging teeth.

American collectors encounter nonlethal species such as the spotted Alphabet Cone *(Conus spurius atlanticus),* the Brown-Banded Mouse Cone *(Conus mus),* and the slender Jasper Cone *(Conus jaspideus)* in the waters off the Florida coast. The rarities, however, originate in the Indo-Pacific waters but are found around the world.

Lozi sorcerors and chiefs in Zambia wore *Conus betulins* pendants as symbols of their special place in the community. The uncommon shells bought slaves as well as status. As late as 1850 the tops of two *C. betulins* paid for one slave. This precious commodity, in the form of cone shell tops, followed a trade route that led inland from the coast. In Angola the cone shells took on a different value; disks fashioned from *Conus prometheus* could not be bought or sold, only handed down from a mother to her daughter. Again, it was a chiefly possession. The royal wives decorated leather-and-brass sashes with the shell disks. Paiwanese politicians of Taiwan also donned cone shell disks to announce their position in society. Commoners could wear them only with special permission.

Yet another twist to the power of the cone shell: Solomon Island chiefs used them in association with auger shells to summon helpful ancestors. Attached to a wooden shield in a geometric pattern, the shells indicated a successful warrior among the Mindanaoan Bagobo people of the Philippines. The Bagobo further used cone shells, specifically cross sections of *C. leopardus,* to make closed-circle bracelets. The perfect shape symbolically formed a barrier against evil.

Sophisticated shell collectors are not without their symbols. The Glory-of-the-Seas Cone *(Conus gloriamaris)* from the southwestern Pacific has become, inadvertently, a status

ONE OF THE MOST COLLECTIBLE families in the shell world, cones are surrounded by mystery, probably in part because they alone within the shell world can be fatal to man.

THESE BARTHELEMYI CONES *(Conus barthelemi)* of the Indian Ocean (below) are not as well known as other Indo-Pacific cones such as the spotted Marble Cone *(C. marmoreus)*, the Geography Cone *(C. geographus)*, and the variable General Cone *(C. generalis)* among others.

symbol for modern shell collectors. Although it is not as rare as it once was, it still commands high prices—sometimes thousands of dollars—at auction. First described in the mid-eighteenth century, this scarce shell numbered fewer than thirty specimens before World War II. Technological advances in underwater exploration—and luck—uncovered more Glory-of-the-Sea Cones, but the shell had already become an icon within the collecting world. No good collection could be without it.

Surprisingly, the Glory-of-the-Sea does not stand out as one of the most beautiful in its family. Its crowded markings seem like white noise compared to the more striking symphonies of other cone shells. Black squares on a white background. Madras bands of yellow and orange. Amber and red tiger stripes. These just begin to describe the variety of patterns within the family.

Stories run rampant when it comes to cone shells, and as with fish stories, the line between reality and fiction easily becomes clouded. One eighteenth-century collector supposedly bid on a Glory-of-the-Seas Cone and rather than placing it next to the one already in his collection, he "crushed it underfoot," writes malacologist R. Tucker Abbott, who also writes that the story was published erroneously. That doesn't stop the tale from circulating as truth!

THE 3- TO 4-INCH (7½- TO 10-cm) Textile Cone (above), is noted for its tentlike markings. Collectors have sometimes confused a large Textile Cone specimen, which is relatively common, with the highly valued collectible, the Glory-of-the-Seas Cone.

AUGERS
(TEREBRIDAE)

Tropical and subtropical shells such as the approximately 150 species of augers flourish in Hawaii, Okinawa, and Florida, among other places. One of the more unusual behaviors in the mollusk world belongs to Salle's Auger *(Hastula salleana),* which in rough water can hoist its foot upward to use as a water sail; the retreating ocean then carries the animal out to sea.

Augers show up in the anthropological record on funerary sticks used in the Solomon Islands. The Common Marlinspike *(Terebra maculata),* found in the Indo-Pacific, symbolized the ancestral powers of the Solomon Islanders. Spirits inhabiting these sticks aided raiding headhunters, chiefs, and others who wanted help from their ancestors.

Collectors often hunt for the Flame Auger *(Terebra taurinus),* with yellowish, orangish, and brown flamelike markings, and for the very slender 3- to 5-inch (7.6- to 12.7-cm) Triple-Banded Auger *(Terebra triseriata)* of the Indo-Pacific. The latter has delicate beaded whorls; if there were a unicorn's horn of the shell world, this would be it.

TURRID SHELLS

The world's largest turrid shell is also one of the world's most interesting. The 3- to 5-inch (7.6- to 12.7-cm) Wonder Shell—also called the Miraculous Thatcher Shell *(Thatcheria mirabilis)*—of Japan bears a series of sharp-edged, ramplike spirals that together embody a grace, elegance, and harmony often associated with the pagodas they closely resemble. The Wonder Shell's unique looks spurred A. Gordon Melvin, author of *Sea Shells of the World,* to write that it is "possibly the most admired of all shells."

THE MIRACULOUS TURRID SHELL of Japan, also known as the Miraculous Thatcher Shell, or simply Miraculous Thatcheria, is one of the world's most beautiful shells. A deepwater animal, it usually grows to between 4 and 5 inches (10 and 12½ cm) tall.

BUBBLE SHELLS
(BULLIDAE)

Approximately thirty species represent the family of true bubble shells. Half a dozen other families, however, include species commonly called bubbles. Classifications can be quite confusing, but most of these related animals possess thin, rounded shells. Japanese waters seem to propagate the most attractive species, among them barely translucent shells such as the boldly striped red-and-white Noble Bubble *(Bullina nobilis)* and the rugby-striped White-Banded Bubble *(Hydatina albocincta).*

In Florida and the Caribbean, collectors often come upon the Common Atlantic Bubble *(Bulla umbilicata),* a shiny, smooth, streaked or striped brown member of the family. Another handsome representative is the Brown-Lined Paper Bubble *(Hydatina vesicaria)* from the same area, a sandy-colored shell crisscrossed by faint reddish and dark-brown wavy lines.

THE CALIFORNIA BUBBLE SHELL (left), an inhabitant of coastal waters from Santa Barbara south, is an ugly duckling compared to some of its American cousins, particularly the Brown-lined Paper Bubble and Sharp's Paper Bubble *(Atys caribaea),* the latter named for the Phrygian fertility god Atys, or Attis.

MALACOLOGISTS SOMETIMES mistakenly classify a shell, a now-and-then occurrence that once affected Common Atlantic Bubble Shells (above), which were listed as *Bulla striata* instead of *Bulla umbilicata.*

© Leland A. Cook

NIIHAU NECKLACES

The island of Niihau lies just off the coast of Kauai in the Hawaiian Islands. Owned by a single family, the island employs only indigenous Hawaiian speakers who respect the traditional old Hawaiian customs. The island is also known for the vast quantities of tiny dove, turban, and rice shells that wash up along its shores. The concentration of skilled craftspeople complements the availability of raw material; Niihau, as a result, has earned a worldwide reputation for its delicate necklaces that appear in art galleries as often as they appear in jewelry stores.

The necklaces reflect the natural beauty of the shells. In many cases, the smaller the shells, the more colorful and valuable the necklaces are. Four shells are commonly used:

Kahelelani shells *(Leptothyra rubricincta)*
Komoa shells *(Turbo intercostalis)*
Momi shells *(Columbella varians)*
Pupu Laiki shells *(Columbella moleculina)*

Within these species, colors vary from white to pink to maroon to blue to orange to brown. There are white shells with black tips, brown spots, or tan stripes; pale blues that almost glow; and a wide range of exquisite yellows. The shells must first be collected, then painstakingly sorted by size and hue, and finally strung. The stringing of the necklaces is, by far, the easiest step in the process. Even the clasp, usually a hook-and-eye arrangement secured to an Isabella or Granulated Cowrie, requires careful handwork.

The simplest Niihau necklace, such as the all-white wedding lei, is a single 60-inch-long (1.5-m) strand of very small white rice shells *(Columbella moleculina)*. The complexity of the Niihau necklaces increases as more and more people express interest in them. The craftspeople create new stringing patterns to make their own mark on the industry and to keep up with modern tastes. Yet the traditional styles are always in demand; some sport a rounded appearance, others look boxy, while still others resemble flowers. Whatever the style, the beauty lies in the shells themselves and in the mystery of their making.

MOST PEOPLE ARE FAMILIAR with the Bivalves (above), a biological class that contains many delicious edible mollusks—clams, mussels, and oysters, to name a few. Bivalves are just beginning to receive serious attention from beginning shell collectors.

Part Two
BIVALVES

ARK SHELLS
(ARCIDAE)

The family of approximately 150 graceful ark shells can be difficult to identify correctly, thus fewer collectors are drawn to them than might be expected. These mostly tropical animals flaunt shells with a beautiful hinge arrangement that in some species resembles the zigzag stitch produced by a sewing machine. Many of the thick, slightly bulbous shells manifest scalloped or toothed edges, and some create a byssus (strong, threadlike strands that attach the shell to rocks or other hard objects); yet one shell's shape, above all, calls the collector's attention to the family. If it were possible to twist a damp shell like a piece of wet laundry, the Twisted Ark *(Trisidos tortuosa)* might be the result. The contorted shell captures the imagination of the collector in a way that few other shells do.

The hills and valleys of the Turkey Wing, or Noah's Ark *(Arca zebra)*, are also striking. Pretty reddish brown bands form a bargello design across its topographic surface. Caribbean fishermen use the 1¾- to 3½-inch (4.4- to 8.9-cm) shell for fish bait, although shellers can find the animal off the eastern coast as far north as the Carolinas.

Nineteenth-century conchologist Charles B. Adams' name graces the small (⅜- to ⅝-inch or .9- to 1.6-cm), finely latticed, yellowish-white Adam's Miniature Ark *(Arcopsis adamsi)* shell, whose almost square interior is captivating.

Scientifically, the most unusual ark shell is, without hesitation, the Blood Ark *(Anadara ovalis* or *Arca ovalis)*, an oddity among the shelled mollusks because it carries hemoglobin, one of the main ingredients in our own blood. Also known as the Bloody Clam, the broad-ridged shell typically rests on sandy and muddy bottoms from the low-tide line to water of about 10 feet (3 m) from Cape Cod to Brazil.

Despite their thick shells, not many ark shells have turned up in archaeological or anthropological annals, although the American Museum of Natural History in New York notes that New Caledonians used *Andara granosa* as a rasp after lashing the shell to a wooden handle.

NOT KNOWING ABOUT THE ANImal that inhabits the shell, most collectors assume that the Blood Ark (right) is ordinary. It is, however, one of the most unusual creatures within the shell world because it is the only species that has red blood (all others have lighter-colored or colorless blood).

MUSSELS
(MYTILIDAE)

Europeans such as Dylan Thomas have had a long-lasting love affair with the mussel that stateside gourmets have missed out on until recently. A mussel farming boom in the Northwest began in the mid-1970s and has helped familiarize Americans with this delicacy. Of the approximately 250 mussel species worldwide, the oblong, edible Blue Mussel *(Mytilus edulis)* dominates both the West and East coasts of the United States.

Waverly Root, in his fascinating book *Food,* attempts to sort out why the Europeans did not continue to eat mussels once they landed on American shores and found the shellfish plentiful. He surmises that the Native Americans, some of whom observed a taboo against mussels, told the colonists to avoid the mollusk. Mussels are known to pick up toxins from their environment, but at the time of colonization the only poison they were exposed to was the tiny organisms of the red tide, which would have rendered the mussels inedible for only a few months of the year. Native Americans on the West Coast learned it was safe to eat mussels when the Pacific equivalent of the red tide (the bloom of dinoflagellates called *Gonyaulax*) dissipated.

Farming mussels has, to a large degree, taken the guesswork out of determining whether the shellfish is edible, and in fact, many aficionados now eat mussels raw with a sprinkle of fragrant vinegar. Having such a close association with humans, mussels do play a role in some legends. One Native American creation myth describes a little boy growing up out of a mussel shell. In 1154, Emperor Frederick

Barbarossa directed his vassals from Liguria (a part of ancient Italy) to bring mussels whenever they visited. Another story tells how mussels saved the life of a Royalist cook during the French Revolution: Employed by the minister of justice who drafted the death sentence for Louis XVI, the cook let slip her political stand in an emotional moment. The minister, however, pardoned her because of her skill at preparing mussels.

The bluish-black color of mussel shells comes not from the shell itself but from the outer "skin" called the periostracum. More practical than aesthetic, mussels do, however, possess a certain beauty most evident in the iridescent interiors of Stearn's, or Adams', Mussel *(Hormomya adamsiana)* of California and the Tulip Mussel *(Modiolus americanus),* whose range stretches from South Carolina to Brazil. The bluish-purple background contrasted with white radial ribs in the Hooked, or Bent, Mussel *(Ischadium recurvum)* seems a parody of a modern jungle print; this pretty departure from the ordinary inhabits waters from Maryland to the Caribbean. All mussels, including Date Mussels, fabricate a byssus, or beard.

Lithophaga, the genus name for Date, or Sea, Mussels, means "eater of rock"—for good reasons; these hardy critters bore into hard clay, mud, coral, and limestone, dissolving obstacles with a secretion of acid. It protects itself with a thick periostracum, which in turn keeps its rich brown shell smooth. The color, smoothness, and extended oblong shape of the Date Mussel reminded early scientists of dates.

THESE BLUE-BLACK MUSSELS from Puget Sound, Washington, share the same niche with white gooseneck barnacles; both cling to surfaces and lead their adult lives in one place.

It was my thirtieth year to heaven
Woke to my hearing from harbour and neighbour wood
And the mussel pooled and the heron
Priested shore.

Dylan Thomas
"Poem in October"

MUSSELS ARE MORE PLENTIFUL
than any other mollusk and
live in densely populated col-
onies, a natural tendency that
man has exploited for his own
uses. Mussel farming is a relatively new industry in the
United States, though Europeans have been raising the edible mollusks for centuries.

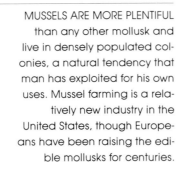

WING AND PEARL OYSTERS
(PTERIIDAE)

In the 1880s, London maintained a society within a society—the street vendors of the East End. Dubbed "Pearlies" because they trimmed their holiday clothing with elaborate designs made with mother-of-pearl buttons, they unwittingly followed a long-standing, worldwide tradition of using the iridescent shell interior and imbuing it with either decorative or symbolic power.

The Igorot people, of Luzon in the Philippines, formed pearly oyster shells into shield-size disks that resembled large buttons; a man wore this status symbol on one hip only if he had successfully taken the head of an enemy. Not until he had completed this task could the young warrior marry.

In Australia, it was believed that a disk made from the Black-Lipped Pearl Oyster *(Pinctada margaritifera)* manipulated evil; the Pitjantjara people assigned to the lustrous circle the power to diagnose and cure sickness. Hand in hand went the belief that a carved point made from the shell could fly through the air and pierce an enemy, causing illness or death. The Pitjantjara also used the shell—which, according to legend, came from mythical creatures—as a part of ritual exchanges.

The shell's lore is rife with associations to magic or power. Among the Mount Hagen people of New Guinea, *P. margaritifera* had the power to attract both valuables and the opposite sex. The shell's powers of attraction extended into the realm of rainmaking; as olive shells supposedly brought the relief of rain to early Mexicans, the pearl oyster watered the earth in Australia.

The glittery iridescence of the pearl oyster's interior lured fish as well, and in many societies fishermen took advantage of the shell's durability and allure and made it into fishhooks. Anthropologists have found pearly fishhooks from the Cook Islands near New Zealand to California.

Considering that the family contains about twenty species, with only six species of tropical pearl oysters, the animals have made a substantial mark on civilization.

A MOLLUSK GENERATES A pearl when a foreign object—a parasite, a grain of sand, even a bit of plastic—enters the inner lining or mantle of the shell. The animal secretes layers of calcium carbonate, which in some shells takes the form of mother-of-pearl, to smooth over the irritating object. The most beautiful pearls come from the Black-lipped Pearl Oyster and the oyster pictured here, the Japanese Oyster *(Pinctada martensi)*.

Why then the world's mine oyster

Which I with sword will open.

William Shakespeare

The Merry Wives of Windsor

HAMMER OYSTERS
(ISOGNOMONIDAE)

"Oysters are more beautiful than any religion.... There's nothing in Christianity or Buddhism that quite matches the sympathetic unselfishness of an oyster," wrote the author Saki (H. H. Munro). His words about the oyster's beauty could pertain to any of the oyster families but are especially apt for hammer oysters.

Also called flat oysters, they make up a family of approximately twenty species that, like their cousins, have a pearly interior area and a byssus. The two T-shaped oysters most commonly recognized as hammer oysters are *Malleus malleus* and *Malleus albus*, the Common and White hammer oysters, both of the Indo-Pacific region. The United States hosts a curious family member that lives in trees, so to speak. The very flat Flat Tree Oyster *(Isognomon alatus)* actually clings to mangrove trees at the low-tide line.

The shells of the hammer oysters, when closed, look like crude picks or hammers; when open, the eye transforms them into birds in flight, moving across the flat surface of a photograph or the tippled terrain of sand.

THE COMMON HAMMER OYSter of the Indo-Pacific generally reaches heights of between 4 and 6 inches (10 and 15 cm). Only a few other members of its immediate family share this unique T-shape, which makes a worthy addition to any general collection.

PEN SHELLS
(PINNIDAE)

Although Edith Hamilton maintains that the mythological Golden Fleece came from a magnificent, magical ram, a few historians surmise that the famous fleece and cloth woven from the golden silk of Pinnidae byssal threads are one and the same. Mediterranean peoples of the ancient world processed the raw material of the pen shells' byssus, carding and spinning it like wool. The resulting cloth was made into articles of clothing, especially gloves and caps. The "sea-silk" became a cherished commodity, in part because, according to R. Tucker Abbott, "a pound of byssus would produce only three ounces (84 g) of high-grade threads." If not protected, the cloth also fell prey to destructive moths, which probably also increased its value. Folklore reveals that Queen Victoria and at least one pope owned a pair of stockings made from the sea silk.

Just under twenty species of *Pinnidae* exist, the largest attaining lengths of more than 2½ feet (76.2 cm). Most have a fan shape that comes down to a point, giving them profiles like those of old-fashioned quill pens. So far no evidence points to use of the pen shell as a writing instrument, but the Andaman Islanders have styled one species, *Atrina vexillum*, into arrowpoints.

WINDOWPANE SHELLS
(PLACUNIDAE)

The Windowpane shell *(Placuna placenta)* looks very much as its name suggests: The shiny, pearly shell can be buffed to near transparency and used for windows or ornamental purposes or, as the Iloko people of Luzon in the Philippines did, as a wind chime to ward off evil spirits. The shells continue as a viable import product, arriving in the United States today as shelly take-offs on Tiffany lampshades.

The Windowpane's relative, the Saddle Oyster *(Placuna sella),* when viewed obliquely, captures the rounded curves of a well-worn saddle. With some imagination, collectors can easily conjure up a ghostly rider sitting side-saddle and galloping off into the waves. The 5- to 10-inch (12.7- to 25.4-cm) Saddle Oyster inhabits the shallow waters of the western Pacific.

OYSTERS

(OSTREIDAE)

In both the Jean La Fontaine fable "The Oyster and the Litigants" (see page 113) and Lewis Carroll's famous poem "The Walrus and the Carpenter," oysters function as objects of greed—yet Charles Dickens wrote, "Poverty and oysters always seem to go together."

In Dickens' day and earlier, oysters were food for poorer classes because they didn't need cooking, and thus used up no fuel. As the populations of underprivileged people grew, oyster beds the world over became depleted. Careful management has revived the industry, but oysters now are considered a rich man's food. In Berlin during World War II, when food for the masses was rationed, delicacies such as caviar and oysters remained within reach of the wealthy, unrestricted but expensive.

The edible oyster's relationship with man goes back to at least neolithic times, when our ancestors devoured enough of the shellfish to leave behind a midden 984 feet long (295 m), 200 feet wide (60 m), and 10 feet deep (3 m) in Western Europe, according to food historian Waverly Root. These ancients dipped into an oyster-laden, 4,000-mile-long (6,400 km) great barrier reef that, Root describes, "started in Scandinavia, ran all the way down the Atlantic coast, turned into the Mediterranean, followed the southern coast of France and the western coast of Italy, passed under the sole of that peninsula, and, losing hardly any oysters to the Adriatic, jumped to Greece . . . where Leander failed and Lord Byron succeeded in swimming the Hellespont." Very, very little of this fertile oyster ground remains.

Stories of great excess involving oysters have drifted down in oral and written tradition. The Roman philosopher and statesman Seneca is said to have eaten one hundred dozen oysters each week. Even in the early 1800s, wrote gourmet Anthelme Brillat-Savarin, diners often consumed twelve dozen oysters each—before dinner. The oysters of the United States have been devoured just as eagerly, and a number of oysters have suffered the same fate as the dodo and the passenger pigeon. Many others are endangered (for example, the small Olympia Oyster of Washington state and the Peconic Oyster of New York). Unfortunately, chemical and thermal pollution have further threatened the shellfish.

The Eastern Oyster (Crassostrea virginica) dominates commercial oyster fisheries in the eastern United States. Its West Coast equivalent is the Giant Pacific Oyster (Crassostrea gigas), which originally came from Japan. To mix matters up further, the predominant European oyster (Ostrea edulis) recently made its debut in American waters. Most varieties that connoisseurs find in restaurants—Chincoteague, Malpeque, and Apalachicola, for instance—are simply the same species—the Eastern Oyster—raised in varied environments. The shells of oysters do assert their own personality from region to region, but on the whole the oyster's appeal lies inside—with its taste—not outside.

One of the more atypical oysters inhabits the waters off southern Florida. The Frons, or Frond, Oyster (Dendrostrea frons) grows an irregularly ridged shell whose spines function as tiny fingers, enabling it to cling to sea whips as koala bears cling to eucalyptus branches. These clasping mollusks, also known as Leafy, or Coon, Oysters, live among hard natural or man-made objects in depths of between two and fifteen feet. Adapting to littered waters, the oysters have been found on cables and wire nets as well as on coral.

But the title of "most unusual family member" goes to the Cock's Comb Oyster (Lopha cristagalli or Ostrea crista-galli), which stands out among all other shells. The angular, lightning-jagged edges on each valve give the impression of a crystalline structure, or perhaps of severely corrugated cardboard. Justly, the shell varies from slate gray to a gray-lavender, the color serving to emphasize the structure.

The Oyster and the Litigants

One day two travelers, walking side by side,
Came on an oyster washed up by the tide.
Greedily they devoured it with their eyes,
Excitedly they pointed out its size,
And then, inevitably, they faced
The problem: which of them as judge
Should pass a verdict on taste?
One was already stooping for the prize
When his friend gave him a nudge:
   "We must decide this properly.
   The epicure's monopoly
Belongs to whoever saw it first: he swallows
The oyster and, it logically follows,
   The other has to watch him do it."
   "If that's the way you view it,
I have, thank God, remarkably keen sight."
   "Mine's pretty good as well,
   And upon my life I swear
I saw it before you!" "So what? All right,
   You may have been
The first to see, but I was the first to smell."

Who should arrive upon this charming scene
But Pierre Dandin? Asked to intervene
   As arbiter in the affair,
   With a portentous air
   He digs the oyster from its shell
And gulps it while his audience stands and stares.
   The meal finished, he declares
In the tone of voice beloved of presidents:
   "The court hereby decrees
An award, without costs, of one shell to each.
   Both parties please
   Proceed without a breach
Of the peace to your lawful residence."

Count what it costs these days to go to court,
And how little the families driven to that resort
Have left after expenses. It's the Law,
It's Pierre Dandin who eats up the rest—
   Who takes the wing and breast
And leaves the litigants the beak and claw.

Jean de la Fontaine (translated by James Michie)

Blonde Aphrodite rose up excited,

Moved to delight by the melody,

White as an orchid she rode quite naked

In an oyster shell on top of the sea.

W. H. Auden

"Anthem for St. Cecilia's Day"

SCALLOPS

(PECTINIDAE)

Unlike Auden, most people conjure up Botticelli's painting *The Birth of Venus* and picture Aphrodite rising up from the sea in a scallop shell. Since she rose from the sea foam, artists presented her as they saw fit, the noble shells—either scallop or oyster—complementing the goddess's beauty. Artists also freely depicted the scallop in religious scenes and in portraits of Saint James.

Saint James' association with the scallop harks back to a legend involving a Spanish nobleman known as the Lord of the Maya. The most consistent story relates that on the way to his wedding the nobleman witnessed what he later called a miracle. His horse bolted into the water and began swimming toward a boat that carried the body of Saint James the Greater. The horse and rider escorted the apostle and came ashore unscathed but covered with scallops. The nobleman quickly converted to Christianity and inadvertently forged the link between scallops, Saint James, and Santiago de Compostela, where the miracle supposedly took place. After pilgrims journeyed to Santiago de Compostela to pay respects to Saint James, they brought back or attached scallop shells to their hats to document the success of their travels, further binding the shell to the place.

Architects frequently borrow the scallop's shape to embellish their structures. From ancient Rome to Victorian England to twentieth-century Spain, the scallop has made its mark on buildings. The shape lent itself to niches for religious artifacts or art; it has appeared as partially domed ceilings in grottoes; and it adorns the exteriors of buildings as varied as the Council on Foreign Relations in New York City and the Casa de las Conchas in Salamanca, Spain.

The scallop motif spread not only via pilgrimages and architecture, but through the use of the shell's image on early coins. In both the fifth and third century B.C. governments issued currency stamped with a picture of *Pecten jacobeus,* Saint James' Scallop.

As life and art became more sophisticated, the scallop's strong design kept inspiring creators, who molded door knockers, salt cellars, and even Rococo-style chairs in the scallop's image—the latter with one "valve" acting as the backrest and the other as the seat.

THE COLORS OF THIS MANTLE Scallop *(Pecten gloripallum)* from the Paumotu Islands just hint at the full palette revealed in a broad collection of scallops.

It follows that scallops took on further religious signifi-cance. During the 1500s, the scallop held a double meaning for devout Spaniards, who used the shell shape as a symbol on their tombstones. Depicted with the hinge, or umbones, right side up, it signified renewed life; represented hinged side down the message was one of divine light. Thousands of miles away in Alaska, Tlingit shamans used noise makers fashioned of overlapping scallop shells *(Pecten caurinus)* to summon spirit helpers.

Most texts estimate the number of scallop species between three hundred and four hundred, although in the United States two species, the Atlantic Bay Scallop *(Argopecten irradians)* and the Atlantic Deep-Sea Scallop *(Placopecten magellanicus),* are most often sought by commercial fisheries.

With the advent of reliable shipping and the trend toward adventurous eating, more species of scallops in the shell are arriving on the tables of American restaurants. Notably, the Singing Scallop *(Chlamys hastata hericus)* has made an appear-ance, steamed and still tucked in its shell with its coral intact.

What we think of as the meat, or eye, of the scallop is the large adductor muscle, which does double-duty work for this tasty mollusk. While most bivalves possess two smaller muscles that open and close the shell, the scallop has only one. This large muscle is partly responsible for the scallop's antics in the water. The *Pecten* scallop moves quite spryly, clapping its two shells together and expelling water through the valves. Born percussionists, these speedy creatures usu-ally wait until they are threatened before they hop away. Their light, strong shells aid their escape; their well-known radial ribbing accounts for the shells' strength. In much deeper water, scallop species lack such pronounced ribs, probably in direct proportion to the decrease of predators in the depths.

MANY OF THE MORE THOR-ough and serious scallop col-lections display only those family members with both valves still attached. The shells shown here (left), nevertheless, would make an interesting dis-play on the variety of scallops.

STRENGTH AND BEAUTY AT-tract collectors to scallops like *Miracpecten mirificus* (below), yet there are other species within the same family with delicate, almost transparent shells.

As anyone familiar with Euell Gibbons' book *Stalking the Blue-Eyed Scallop* knows, scallops have eyes. And ears. Situated along the mantle's edges, the light-sensitive eyes detect shadows that inform the scallop of a possible predator. The ears are simply the triangular extensions near the hinge at the bottom of the shell.

Generally shell connoisseurs stay away from bivalves—with the exception of scallops and some oysters. The range of colors and augmented shapes make them one of the more intriguing bivalve families to collect. The Glorious Scallop *(Pecten gloriosus)* of Australia and the popular Noble Scallop *(Pecten nobilis* or *Chlamys nobilis)* of Japan boast beautiful tropical and pastel colors: oranges, yellows, or purples.

In American waters, the Lion's Paw *(Lyropecten nodosus)* is a much-sought-after, many-frilled and fanned collector's item. The simple but pretty dark-against-light Calico Scallop *(Argopecten gibbus)* commonly washes up on Caribbean beaches, but the most dazzling scallops inhabit the waters of Indo-Pacific province, among them the deep-water Asian Moon Scallop *(Amusium pleuronectes)*, which forms a white bottom shell (or valve) and a colored top shell; the Sun-and-Moon Scallop *(Amusium japonicum)*; and the red-splotched Folded Scallop *(Decatopecten plica)*, which is smaller and shaped more like a teardrop pearl.

ONE OF THE MORE UNUSUAL aspects of the Lion's Paw (left) is the difference between its two valves or shell halves. The photograph of the Atlantic Bay Scallop (right) focuses not on the shell itself but on the scallop's bright blue, light-sensitive eyes.

Demo

ESTIMATES PLACE ABOUT 65 species of scallop within range of the United States. These shells (following page, left), probably beach finds, originated near Yaquina Bay on the Oregon Coast. The Flame Scallop *(Lima scabra)* (following page, right) photographed off Roatan, Honduras, comes from an area famed for its underwater flora and fauna. Scuba divers turned Roatan into a destination resort perfect for watching shells in their native habitat.

© Alex Kerstitch

Give me my scallop-shell of quiet,

My staff of faith to walk upon,

My scrip of joy, immortal diet,

My bottle of salvation,

My gown of glory, hope's true gage,

And thus I'll take my pilgrimage.

Sir Walter Raleigh

"The Passionate Man's Pilgrimage"

The Oyster

The oyster's a confusing suitor;

It's masc., and fem., and even neuter.

At times it wonders, may what come,

Am I husband, wife, or chum.

Ogden Nash

THORNY OYSTERS

(SPONDYLIDAE)

This small but well-collected family includes only one genus with approximately forty tropical species. The shells' spiny projections, which sometimes extend as much as 1 foot (30.5 cm) or more and can double the length of the shell, encouraged more than the usual complement of common names, among them chrysanthemum shell, thorny oyster, and rock oyster. Although not related to the true oyster, they are similar in that they remain attached to a solid base—coral, ocean debris, or occasionally even another oyster—throughout their lives.

These oysters are surprisingly beautiful in both shape and color. The scope ranges through simple whites, dips into yellows and oranges, and boldly goes on to reds and purples. With a squint of the eyes, the shell may look something like a modern dancer's costume, the spines resembling tubed fringes of material hanging down at odd lengths, the colors running into a background of white. Or, the shell may look like a dandelion in the fluff stage or like an eponymous chrysanthemum.

Peruvians of 900 B.C. appreciated the shell's novelty and created pottery that mimicked its shape. Tombs hold more evidence of the pre-Columbians' affinity for the shell, as does a sixteenth-century text, the Codex Mendoza, which describes a tribute to the emperor Montezuma of eight hundred shells, probably American Chrysanthemum shells *(Spondylus americanus).*

ALTHOUGH THE AMERICAN Chrysanthemum Shell (left) is also known descriptively as the Atlantic Thorny Oyster, that cognomen more deservedly should go to the spiky *Spondylus aurantium* (below). Despite their name, thorny oysters are not close kin to true oysters.

JEWEL BOX SHELLS
(CHAMIDAE)

The jewel box shells' history in the Indo-Pacific Islands begins most likely with the evidence found in kitchen middens. As with other attractive edible shells, man turned from using the Chamidae exclusively for food to using the shells ritually. In the Solomon Islands as recently as the last decade or so, armbands made from Chamidae could be exchanged—not bought—ceremonially, primarily as bride-wealth. The islanders, like other peoples throughout the world, perceived the shells—and objects made from them—as articles of status. On one island the women went so far as to make money disks from *Chama* shells.

A medium-size family whose most notable members inhabit tropical waters, Chamidae shells inspire whimsical comparisons. The translucent Clear Jewel Box *(Chama arcana)*, for instance, looks like a young girl's layered crinoline. If a head of lettuce became encrusted with colorful calcareous material, it just might resemble the Leafy Jewel Box *(Chama macerophylla)*, whose range of hues—with only a little exaggeration—rivals that of the best crayon companies. One might call the Lazarus Jewel Box *(Chama lazarus)* the shell of a hundred tongues, although its many protrusions probably number less than that.

Most of the species, like the thorny oysters, live in quiet waters and attach themselves to rocks, wrecks, corals, and other hard surfaces, so they can maintain long spines or fronds that under different environmental conditions would break off. Each side of the shell, or each valve, tends to differ in size and shape, one of the quirks of the family.

Flaunting beauty, ceremonial value, and taste, the Chamidae are also of scientific interest. Of the dozen-plus species that live off the coasts of the United States, the Leafy Jewel Box and its smaller relation, the Little Corrugated Jewel Box *(Chama congregata)*, share the same habitat from North Carolina to Brazil. While the larger species favors rocks and solid debris, the smaller often affixes itself to pen shells—a small-scale illustration of what biologists call adaptive radiation, a principle by which similar animals find different environmental niches.

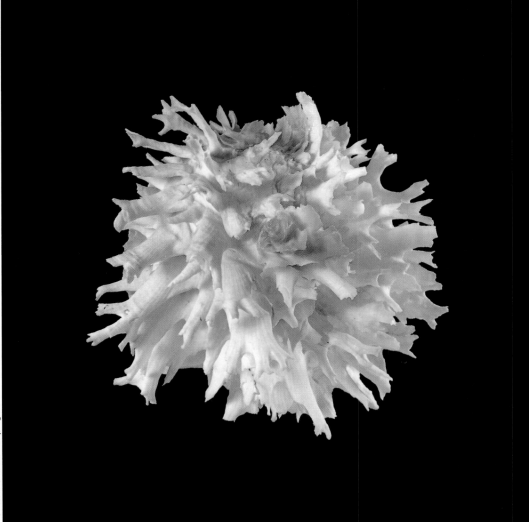

FRILLY AND COLORFUL FOR THE most part, jewel box shells prefer rocky or hard surfaces for their habitats, sometimes growing up on coral, wrecks, even other (dead) shells. Collectors can easily miss these shells when searching underwater for them because algae, worm tubes, and other growths often inadvertently act as camouflage.

CARDITAS

(CARDITIDAE)

Texts vary in their classifications, placing between thirty and two hundred species in the family Carditidae.

Many of these Carditidae shells have a quiet, unpretentious attractiveness that appeals to collectors as surely as the gaudy flamboyance of the jewel boxes. The striping on the tawny Carpenter's Cardita *(Glans subquadrata)* and the brownish gray Broad-Ribbed, or Florida, Cardita *(Carditamera floridana)* leaves an impression of plumage, especially when the two valves are displayed together. The oddly angled oblong Carditidae "wings" sport concentric bands of color that appear to ride over the thick, bumpy ribs. One of the flashiest members of the family is the western Pacific Rosy Cardita *(Cardita crassicosta),* a nubby-spined shell of varying colors.

In contrast, the Domingo Cardita *(Glans dominguensis)* seems light and airy; its whitish shell gleams with a rosy iridescence when fresh. Neither it nor its cousin, the Carpenter's Cardita, live up to the genus name, which derives from the Latin word for acorn.

COCKLES

(CARDIIDAE)

The cockles of Mary's garden are shelled gymnasts capable of jumping several inches. A powerful foot energizes these ribbed charmers. Their attractiveness lies in their variety—from the romantically shaped, delicate Heart Cockle *(Corculum cardissa)* to the Ribbed, or Costate, Cockle *(Cardium costatum).* With its bold, almost clawlike ribbings and broad body, the latter, a warm-water West African shell, looks like a sculptor's exaggerated rendering.

Oblong, heart-shaped, fan-shaped, or round, cockles are common the world over, and they've become a part of folklore not just in nursery rhymes, but also in myths and medicinal tradition. The Tlingit people of the Northwest Coast of the United States believed that the first humans arose from the machinations of a raven and a cockle or clam. On the other side of the earth, in the Far East, shells, including cockles, told Andaman Islanders that a person's soul had successfully made the transition from life to death (see also tusk shells, page 58). Whether noted in cockles or leaves, the heart shape directed medicine men in some cultures to use these offerings from nature as a potion for curing heart problems.

THE SEA'S VALENTINES, 3-INCH (7½-cm) Heart Cockles (near right) from the Philippines are much more graceful than these Pink Cockles (far right) from Sanibel Island, Florida, that are large enough to hold a pink crab.

Mary, Mary, quite contrary

How does your garden grow?

With silver bells and cockle shells,

And pretty maids all in a row

      Nursery rhyme

Love's feeling is more soft and sensible
Than are the tender horns of cockled snails.

William Shakespeare
Love's Labor's Lost

The Heart Cockle illustrates an interesting evolutionary lesson. Because the genus developed a shape that prevented normal formation of a siphon and burrowing in sand, these cockles remain fixed and immovable on coral reefs. As an illustration of how nature provides for its creatures, the Heart Cockle's shell is quite thin—so thin, in fact, that sunlight infiltrates the shell and attracts a nonthreatening, nourishing algae.

Europeans still eat the cockles celebrated in the Molly Malone song: "Cockles and mussels, alive, alive-o!" And a few people in the United States dine on Giant Pacific *(Trachycardium quadrigenarium)* and Giant Atlantic, or Great Heart *(Dinocardium robustum),* cockles and Nuttall's Cockle *(Clinocardium muttali).* Do not be misled by the common names; the giants rarely reach more than 5 inches (12 cm) in length. In comparison with the approximately two hundred other species throughout the world, however, the giants are huge; the smallest cockles measure only about ⅛ inch (.3 cm).

SIZE IS ALWAYS RELATIVE: THE Giant Atlantic Cockle of the southeastern United States measures only about 5¼ inches (13 cm) at its largest, a giant compared to other American cockles that grow no larger than ⅛ inch (⅓ cm).

SURF CLAMS

(MACTRIDAE)

Although surf clams—or trough clams, as they are sometimes called—are not on collectors' top-forty lists, they often end up in chowder and other processed foods. These are the plain Janes of the shell world.

Harvested along the Georges Bank, the Atlantic Surf Clam *(Spisula solidissima)* may not be aglimmer with iridescent hues, but its range of names is colorful. According to *The Audubon Society Field Guide to North American Seashells,* the people of the mid-Atlantic states refer to *S. solidissima* as the Beach Clam or Skimmer Clam. In Maine, it's the Hen Clam, while Canadians call it the Bar Clam.

THIS ATLANTIC SURF CLAM (left), photographed at Fire Island, New York, is a member of an unassuming family often overlooked by collectors. The clam is much more well known for its tasty flesh. Found just below the surface at beyond the low-tide line to 140 feet (42 m), it is accessible to novice clammers and commercial fishermen.

SANIBEL ISLAND BOASTS A worldwide reputation as a sheller's paradise primarily because of its wide variety of gastropods, yet this clam (above) shows that the waters off Sanibel also host lowly clams.

IN THE WILD, THESE TRIDACNA clams (above) from Palau flaunt their beautiful colors. Although Giant Clams have been known to produce golf-ball-sized pearls, they lack the luster of oyster pearls. Their attractiveness to man lies in their size and color, not in their pearls.

GIANT CLAMS
(TRIDACNIDAE)

The heavyweight champion of the shell world is without a doubt the Giant Clam *(Tridacna gigas)*. This molluscan behemoth can weigh in at ½ ton (.45 m) and measure more than 4 feet (1.2 m) long.

These huge shells have been put to many uses by man, including bathtubs (an engraving shows a mother in the Molucca Islands bathing her child in one), sinks (in the famed Coco Palms Hotel in Kauai), and feeding troughs; the shell is so strong that it has also been used as an ax head for felling trees.

In *20,000 Leagues Under the Sea,* Jules Verne mentions a fountain made from a Giant Clam shell measuring "about thirty-five feet (10 m) around its delicately scalloped rim. It was even larger than those lovely giant clams given to Francis I by the Republic of Venice, and which the church of Saint-Sulpice in Paris has made into two huge holy-water basins."

The horror stories of pearl divers being eaten by the overweight shells are merely legend. The animal barely opens its valves enough to let water in, let alone a chunky arm or leg. And if a person did insert a limb, the mollusk would give warning by closing its shells only part of the way, giving the intruder time enough to extricate himself. This gentle giant, surprisingly enough, is a vegetarian.

The family also includes the divine *Tridacna squamosa,* which grows to 16 inches (40.6 cm). Subtle pastel colors enhance the sculpted, fluted shell, and its delicacy rather than its size makes it lovely.

The Bear's Paw *(Hippopus hippopus)* also falls within this family. In Bali these shells, whose two valves are unusually deep, were used as the vessel portion of an oil lamp.

THESE BEHEMOTHS ARE actually vegetarians that feed on symbiotic algae that live within their mantles. The creatures might even be thought of as benevolent, because fish and other living things use the shells for protection, food, or shelter.

TELLINS

(TELLINIDAE)

At the turn of the century a young girl coming out in society might have worn a trembler, a delicate wreath of small white rice shells and pink-tinged rose tellins. As the girl walked, the circlet quivered, or trembled, from her movement. From afar the shells looked like baby's breath and sweetheart roses.

More than two hundred shells make up this mostly tropical family that is known scientifically for its separate intake and outflow siphons. The long intake siphon cuts through the sandy or muddy habitat into the food-enriched water; the shorter siphon eliminates waste. This arrangement, coupled with the animal's horizontal (not vertical) orientation, are adaptations to the shifting sands of their environment.

Some of the shells' common names give clues to the family's most attractive members. The rays of the pink and yellow Sunrise Tellin *(Tellina radiata)* form a sunburst, as do the bands on the Indo-Pacific *Tellina variegata*. Put a pink-striped Candy Stick Tellin *(Tellina similis)* in a sweetshop, and it could easily fool customers into believing that some enterprising entrepreneur had fashioned peppermint drops into a small clamshell shape.

Collectors find the colors and fragility of tellin shells attractive. Although some authorities classify tellins as living only within Indo-Pacific waters, others maintain that the family has representatives in the Caribbean (for example, the Candy Stick Tellin) and the Mediterranean (the Hatchet Tellin).

One of the most common tellins along the southern Atlantic coast, the Alternate Tellin *(Tellina alternata)*, is also called the Lined Tellin because its real beauty—bands of delicate color—lies inside the shells. The smooth, glossy, sometimes deep-pink interior of the Rose Petal Tellin *(Tellina lineata)*, another southeastern species, rates highly among designers of shell crafts, who use the shell in pictures or assemblages of molluscan bouquets. Dall's Dwarf Tellin *(Tellina sybaritica)* takes its species name from the same root as the word *sybarite*; both refer to the notorious richness and luxury of Sybaris, the ancient Greek city in southern Italy that fell in 510 B.C. On first glance the little shell (about ¼ inch or .6 cm long) seems white or translucent, but its true nature is more opalescent than milky.

WEDGE CLAMS
(DONACIDAE)

People call the celebrity of the family Donacidae by many names, but the most common names are coquinas and butterfly shells. Field guides describe *Donax variabilis* as "elongately triangular, wedge-shaped," which means that the shells are shaped like a triangle of dough that's been pushed in. The unflattering interpretation belies the shell's splendor.

Wet, sandy ground provides prime habitat for these intertidal animals. In their finest form, the coquinas sport madras-patterned shells in colors as varied as orange and purple, blue and brown, or pink and yellow. A row of fine teeth sometimes marks the interior edge of the shells.

Although they are not exploited commercially, coquinas make a good soup base and are frequently dug for their meat.

BUTTERFLY SHELLS, OR COQUI-nas, inhabit many temperate and tropical beaches. The best time to see them in action is when the tide is coming in; these colorful animals come to the surface to feed as the waves travel up sandy beaches. At other times they are hidden just below the surface with their siphons sticking out of the moist sand.

FOREIGN COUSIN TO THE
American Hard Shell Clam
or Quahog, the 1-to 2-inch
(3-to 5-cm) Camp Pitar Venus
(Lioconcha castrensis) hails
from the Indo-Pacific.

VENUS CLAMS
(VENERIDAE)

This large family, with almost five hundred species worldwide, encompasses many of the most well-known edible clams, among them quahogs, littlenecks, the Frilled Californian Venus *(Chione undatella),* butter clams, and the Pismo Clam *(Tivela stultorum).*

Most Easterners, if not most Americans, know the Northern Quahog *(Merceneria merceneria* or *Venus merceneria).* In its most youthful incarnation, *M. merceneria* goes by the name littleneck. As it grows, connoisseurs call it a cherrystone clam. By the time it reaches adulthood, its meat toughening with age, the Northern Quahog becomes known as the chowder clam, or Quahog.

It's easy to overlook the fineness of the venus clams. People generally come into contact with the prosaic edible clams. Branching out, however, introduces beginners to such stunning shells as the Wedding Cake Venus *(Callanaitis disjecta)* of Australia, the Pacific Comb Venus *(Pitar lupinaria),* and the Leafy Venus *(Venus rosalina)* from Africa. Each name fits the shells well. If one were to decorate a 1½- to 2-inch (3.8- to 5.1-cm) shell in broad bands of white chocolate, allowing the edges of each band to curl up at a slight angle, the Wedding Cake Venus would be the result. The sense of modeled material—whether chocolate, frosting, or clay—is the essence of the Leafy Venus. When viewed from the side, each layer looks like a small, leafy edge. In contrast, the bold Pacific Comb Venus might double as an Amazon's spined breast shield. The image of delicacy in one species evolves into one of robust power in another.

Not all of the approximately five hundred species are beautiful, and not all of the beautiful species have a sculpted quality. A few species owe their comeliness to intricate patterns that seem woven into the smooth-sided shells. Specimens of the Lettered Venus *(Tapes litterata),* for example, can exhibit tentlike or rayed markings and even patterns that look as if they had jumped off a seismograph. More subtle patterns show up on the eastern species called Gould's Waxy Clam *(Gouldia cerina).*

The Sunray Venus *(Macrocallista nimbosa),* with its woven-bag design, is one of the prettier edible species. The smooth and sometimes discreetly rayed lines along the surface of the Pismo Clam also makes it a pretty mollusk for the table. The population of these flavorful creatures has declined from overharvesting; however, individuals can sometimes still dig a small number of these clams per day.

The Clam

The clam, esteemed by gourmets highly,

Is said to live the life of Riley;

When you are lolling on a piazza

It's what you are as happy as a.

                    Ogden Nash

ANGEL WINGS AND PIDDOCKS
(PHOLADIDAE)

The lovely Angel Wing *(Cyrtopleura costata)* does indeed recall the shape and lightness of a wing. A certain twist gives the 4- to 8-inch (10.2- to 20.3-cm) shell motion, and the hinge of the two valves—the umbones—at one end leaves the "wings" ready for flight. One could almost slip the wings on and take off. On close inspection, the dominant ribbing appears to be made of a vertical line of small scales; the overall effect is highly sculpted and classically beautiful.

Although some West Indians find the flesh of Angel Wings tasty, most of the people who seek these creatures are shell collectors. Enthusiasts can uncover these prizes from New Jersey south to the northern Caribbean and west to the coast of Texas.

The family of about one hundred species distinguishes itself primarily because, while alive, they possess what malacologists call accessory plates—shelly growths that cover and protect the area around the umbones and the animal's muscle. Since the piddock family members are borers, the muscles take on greater importance. These burrowers assault not just mud and wood but also soft rock and even lead and plastic cables.

SHIPWORMS
(TEREDINIDAE)

Approximately sixty species comprise this family of wood borers. The small shells (about ¼ inch or .6 cm long)—which are attached to a limy tube secreted by the creature's mantle—furnish no clues as to species or genera; classification depends, instead, on study and comparison of the "pallets" at the animal's rear end. The pallets can take either a paddlelike or many-feathered shape and serve to close off the shelly tube.

Optimists might say that these are helpful creatures, eating away the old, cast-off pieces of wood that commonly litter harbors. Wooden boat owners would heartily disagree, calling shipworms destructive pests, for they invade the wood when young and barely noticeable, then they eat their way from the inside out, leaving only a small siphon open to view.

THE WHITE, TEXTURED BEAUTY of Angel Wings doesn't give a clue to its nature. Far from living out it's life delicately, this Piddock shell is a borer, carving out a niche for itself in sandstone and other hard materials.

PEARLY TALES

The lore of pearls almost rivals the lore of the sea. Whispered stories circulate with certain pearls, as with gemstones. Many stories associate these sea jewels with legendary and historic celebrities, but perhaps the most famous tales are those that surround the four large, teardrop pearls that grace the Imperial State Crown in the Tower of London. One tale weaves its plot around Queen Elizabeth I, who had them set as earrings; another story claims that three of the pearls belonged at one time to the renowned Hanoverian Pearls given to Catherine de Medici by the pope. Catherine supposedly passed the Hanoverian Pearls to her daughter-in-law, Mary, Queen of Scots, from whom Elizabeth I acquired them. Succession passed them next to King James I; then to his daughter Elizabeth of Bohemia; on down to her daughter Sophia; and then to Sophia's son, who became King George I. Today, both the Queen Mother and Queen Elizabeth II have necklaces fashioned from the celebrated pearls.

Any of the approximately fifty species of Ostreidae oysters could produce pearls, which are simply layers of shelly material secreted by the mantle over a foreign object that has found its way into the shell. Pearls, however, take on the appearance of the "mother" (the interior surface of the shell), and the pearls of many species would lack the luster—and thus the value—of those produced by *Pinctada* oysters. Pinna shells sometimes produce black pearls, while the Pink Conch can form pink pearls.

ALMOST ALL SHELLS HAVE THE capability of generating a pearl, but only the *Pinctada* oysters have the luster to produce fine pearls for quality jewelry. Within the oyster family, the differing species produce a dazzling array of subtly hued pearls—from gray to black to cream to white.

SHELL CLUBS

Listed below is a representative sample of shell clubs in North America. Most of the addresses change from year to year as the clubs' officers change. The best, most up-to-date listings are included every year in the first or second issue of the *American Malacological Bulletin;* the bulletin, unfortunately, also has no permanent office, but is available at many natural history museum libraries. Call your local museum first to see if they have information about local shell groups. There are no organized shell clubs in Canada. However, if you contact your local museum, you will probably be able to find other enthusiasts in your area.

The list below includes the name of each shell club and, if not indicated in the name, the area it covers.

Conchologists of America

The Austin (Texas) Shell Club

Boston Malacological Club, Inc.

Chicago Shell Club

Coastal Bend Shell Club
(Corpus Christi Museum, Texas)

Greater Miami Shell Club, Inc.

The Greater St. Louis Shell Club

Hawaiian Malacological Society

Houston Conchology Society

Jacksonville (Florida) Shell Club, Inc.

Jersey Cape (New Jersey) Shell Club

Long Island Shell Club, Inc.

Louisiana Malacological Society

Louisville Conchological Society

Marco Island (Florida) Shell Club

Minnesota Society of Conchologists

Naples (Florida) Shell Club

National Capital Shell Club (Washington, D.C.)

North Carolina Shell Club

New York Shell Club, Inc.

North Texas Conchological Society

Northern California Malacozoological Club

Palm Beach County (Florida) Shell Club

Philadelphia Shell Club

St. Petersburg (Florida) Shell Club

San Antonio (Texas) Shell Club

San Diego (California) Shell Club

Sanibel-Captiva (Florida) Shell Club

Sarasota (Florida) Shell Club

Seashell Searchers of Brazoria County (Texas)

South Carolina Shell Club

Southwest Florida Conchologist Society, Inc.

Southwestern Malacological Society (Arizona)

Western Society of Malacologists (California)

FOR FURTHER READING

Abbott, R. Tucker. *American Seashells.* New York: Van Nostrand Reinhold Co., 1974 (second edition).

Abbott, R. Tucker. *Kingdom of the Seashell.* New York: Bonanza Books, 1982.

Abbott, R. Tucker. *Seashells of the World: A Guide to the Better-Known Species.* New York: Golden Press, 1985.

Arthur, Alex. *Shells: An Eyewitness Guide.* New York: Alfred A. Knopf, 1989.

Dance, S. Peter. *The World's Shells: A Guide for Collectors.* New York: McGraw-Hill Book Company, 1976.

Gibbons, Euell. *Stalking the Blue-Eyed Scallop.* New York: David McKay, 1964.

Hodgson, Martha Keeling. *The Spell of the Shell.* New York: Hawthorn Books, 1975.

Rehder, Harrold A. *The Audubon Society Field Guide to North American Seashells.* New York: Alfred A. Knopf, 1981.

Root, Waverly. *Food: An Authoritative and Visual History and Dictionary of the Foods of the World.* New York: Simon and Schuster, 1980.

Safer, Jane Frearer and Frances McLaughlin Gill. *Spirals From the Sea: An Anthropological Look at Shells.* New York: Clarkson N. Potter, 1982.

Stix, Hugh, Marguerite Stix, and R. Tucker Abbott. *The Shell: Five Million Years of Inspired Design.* New York: Abradale Press, 1988.

Travers, Louise Allerdice. *The Romance of Shells in Nature and Art.* New York: M. Barrows, 1962.

Ward, Peter Douglas. *In Search of Nautilus: Three Centuries of Scientific Adventures in the Deep Pacific to Capture a Prehistoric—Living—Fossil.* New York: New York Academy of Sciences, 1988.